Heavenly Treasures

May the Lord bless
your heart and life
as you read!

In His Grace,

Glenna

Phil. 1:6

Heavenly Treasures

Discovering the
Sovereign Grace
of God Hidden
in the Richness of
His Word

GLENNA SALSBURY

REDEMPTION PRESS

Published by Redemption Press, PO Box 427, Enumclaw, WA 98022

All Scripture quotations, unless otherwise indicated, are taken from the *Holy Bible: King James Version.*

Scripture quotations marked NIV are taken from the *Holy Bible, New International Version®, NIV®.* Copyright © 1973, 1978, 1984 by Biblica, Inc.™ Used by permission of Zondervan. All rights reserved worldwide. www.zondervan.com

Scripture quotations marked NLT are taken from the *Holy Bible, New Living Translation,* copyright © 1996. Used by permission of Tyndale House Publishers, Inc., Wheaton, IL 60189 USA. All rights reserved.

Scripture quotations marked NASB are taken from the *New American Standard Bible,* © Copyright 1960, 1962, 1963, 1968, 1971, 1972, 1973, 1975, 1977 by The Lockman Foundation. Used by permission.

Scripture quotations marked "TLB" or "The Living Bible" are taken from The Living Bible [computer file] / Kenneth N. Taylor.—electronic ed.—Wheaton : Tyndale House, 1997, c1971 by Tyndale House Publishers, Inc. Used by permission. All rights reserved.

Revised Standard Version of the Bible, copyright 1952 [2nd edition, 1971] by the Division of Christian Education of the National Council of the Churches of Christ in the United States of America. Used by permission. All rights reserved.

ISBN 13: 978-1-63232-078-0
Library of Congress Catalog Card Number: 2008908936

Dedication

To the great saints of old who loved the Word of God with all their hearts.

To Charles Haddon Spurgeon (1834–1892), England's "Prince of Preachers" whose *Morning and Evening* devotionals have fed my spirit for more than four decades.

To the apostle Paul, whose writings reveal the mystery of grace and whose grasp on the sovereignty of God is unparalleled.

To the Holy Spirit, the One Who leads us into all truth and anoints our minds and hearts with understanding.

To the Lord Jesus Christ, Who called me out of darkness into His glorious light and gave me a hunger for His Word.

Contents

SANCTIFICATION

SOVEREIGNTY

ENCOURAGEMENT

SIGNPOSTS TO THE SAVIOR

HEAVEN

Preface

Lay not up for yourselves treasures on earth...
but lay up for yourselves treasures in heaven...
for where your treasure is, there will your heart be also.
—Matthew 6:19-21

I have often pondered over these verses, asking myself, "How? What is the best way to lay up treasures in heaven? How might I do that?"

Certainly there are a variety of meaningful responses to that question. But here is the one that rings most true in my heart. Peter wrote, quoting Isaiah, "The Word of the Lord endures forever" (1 Peter 1:25). For me, digging out the treasures of His Word and storing them in my heart answers the "how" question.

"Heaven and earth shall pass away: but my words shall not pass away" (Luke 21:33). It is only the Word that endures forever. Even heaven and earth will pass away! And the Word is powerful, life-giving. It is likened to the heavenly manna given to sustain the Israelites on a daily basis.

Jesus taught the disciples to ask Him for daily bread. He meant more than physical food when He taught them to pray like that.

In the gospel of John we hear Him say, "I am the bread of life.... This is the bread that comes down from heaven, that a man eat thereof and not die" (John 6:48, 50). Again He says, "If ye continue in my Word then are ye my disciples indeed; And ye shall know the truth and the truth shall make you free."

The Scripture is life-giving and joy-restoring. Faith comes to us by the Word of God. I need fresh life, daily doses of joy, and a lot more faith! How about you? The thrill of discovering the riches of the Word of God is addicting and transformational.

Having said all that, the question often remains, "But how can I actually absorb the Word?"

I have personally experienced the answer to that question. Soaking up the Word of God happens best when I ask the Lord to shine His light on just a verse or two. There are gems of truth hidden in every single line of the Scripture. The Spirit speaks to our spirit as we listen for His voice and meditate on a particular passage.

Every treasure in the pages that follow has been a result of the Spirit revealing the richness of the Word to my heart. I believe you will be deeply moved by listening as His Spirit speaks to you, treasure upon treasure.

Perhaps the most uplifting experience you will have is to hear His voice and record what personal thought or revelation He gives you as you absorb each of the writings that follow.

The Lord spoke to me one cold January morning as I was reading and loving a devotional by Charles Spurgeon. He pointed out that I could enhance my own life in Christ by recording the gems of insight He was giving me, day after day, year after year. He then prompted me to step out in faith and share these as weekly online devotionals.

Now, after several years, many of you continue to share with me the encouragement you have received through these treasures. You have often said a particular truth arrived on the day you desperately needed to hear it. And, of course, that is how the Spirit comforts us, in His sovereign timing.

It is my heart's desire that you will spend years reading and rereading these treasures. The Word of God is alive, coming to us afresh every time we read a familiar passage.

It is my prayer that your experience with this book will be transformational. May He use these words to answer your heart's desire to store up treasures in heaven. And may your longing to know Him better be fulfilled as you ponder His Word as found on the pages that follow.

In His love,
Glenna

Grace

And if by grace, then it is no more of works;
otherwise grace is no more grace.
—Romans 11:6a

Masterpiece of God's Grace

Not by works of righteousness which we have done,
but according to His mercy He saved us,
by the washing of regeneration,
and renewing of the Holy Ghost,
which He shed on us abundantly,
through Jesus Christ our Savior.
—Titus 3:5-6

Oh, the mystery of the grace that God the Father poured out on those whom He has called unto Himself. Again and again in Scripture we see that the miraculous experience of life in Christ is based on His work alone. We, as recipients of His grace, have not contributed one element to our salvation. "Not by works of righteousness which we have done."

Even our faith in Him, our believing, is a gift. The love of God is shed abroad in our hearts by the Holy Spirit (Romans 5:5). No human being seeks after God. No, not one (Romans 3:11). He is the One Who has come to seek and to save us (Luke 19:10).

Consider again the words Paul wrote to Titus, "He has saved us according to His mercy." How did the Father save us? By the cleansing, renewing work of His Spirit, which He shed on us abundantly through the work of His Son, Jesus Christ.

Oh, how the saints of old treasured the truths of the grace and mercy of our sovereign God. It was John Newton, a slave ship captain who came to know Christ as an adult, (on March 10, 1748, in a brutal storm) who penned the words: "Amazing grace! How sweet the sound! That saved a wretch like me! I once was lost, but now am found; was blind, but now I see."

Charles Wesley, on Tuesday, May 23, 1738, wrote the words of the hymn, "And Can It Be That I Should Gain?" The last verse says, "Long my imprisoned spirit lay, Fast bound in sin and nature's night; Thine eye diffused a quickening ray, I woke, the dungeon flamed with light; My chains fell off, my heart was free; I rose, went forth and followed thee."

The apostle Paul continually wrote of the grace of God. He reminded the saints in Ephesus, "Once you were dead, doomed forever because of your many sins…But God is so rich in mercy, and He loved us so very much, that even while we were dead He gave us life…(It is only by God's special favor that you have been saved)" (Ephesians 2:1, 4, 5 NLT).

One of the great realities about the grace of God in bringing us to Himself is that He has a purpose for us. We have been saved and will live forever as trophies of His grace and His kindness. "For we are God's masterpiece. He has created us anew in Christ Jesus so that we can do the good things He planned for us long ago" (Ephesians 2:10 NLT) "And so God can always point to us as examples of the incredible wealth of His favor and kindness toward us…" (Ephesians 2:7 NLT).

And so, our lives are in His hands. And, it is all about Him… not about us. Praise His name!

Father, we continually praise You for Your mercy. Grant us the ability to give You all the glory.

The Righteousness of Christ

*…not having mine own righteousness, which is of the law,
but that which is through the faith of Christ….*
—Philippians 3:9

The apostle Paul had a pedigree that qualified him for human accolades. He was a Roman citizen, a circumcised Jew from the tribe of Benjamin, a Bible scholar, a law-keeping Pharisee, and a zealous religious leader in Israel. Yet Paul discovered that nothing in his humanity contributed to his standing in God's eyes. "But what things were gain to me, those I counted loss for Christ" (Philippians 3:7).

Paul had been given the revelation of God's amazing grace, the only instrument by which we are born again. It was Paul who wrote, "There is none righteous, no not one. There is none that understandeth, there is none that seeketh after God" (Romans 3:10-11). (And Paul was quoting Old Testament truths from Psalm 14, Psalm 53, and passages in Isaiah.)

Let's think about this together. No human being (who is not alive in Christ) ever seeks God. In the flesh, in the natural human condition, no one ever seeks God. And all of man's human attempts to "shape up" or earn God's favor are useless because God will not look upon sin. In fact, the apostle John told us that God does not even hear the prayers of sinners—those who do not know Him (John 9:31). And all human beings are sinners. Isn't it strange that as evangelicals we refer to "the sinner's prayer"? No one can pray the prayer for salvation who isn't already alive in the Spirit! "No man can come to me except the Father who hath sent me, draw him..." (John 6:44).

This scenario is a hopeless dilemma, humanly speaking. God is righteous; God is perfect; God will only have a relationship with righteous, perfect people. And there are no perfect people to be found. "All have sinned and come short of the glory of God" (Romans 3:23).

How, then, is it possible for us to enter into the Lord's presence to have a relationship with Him? In Hebrews we read, "Without faith it is impossible to please God" (Hebrews 11:6). The key is that the miracle of entering the presence of God is based on faith: the belief that Christ is God in the flesh, and the belief that Christ's righteousness, His sinlessness, counts for me. But whose faith is it that opens up this way into God's presence?

The apostle Paul answered the question in the Philippians 3:9 quote. Through the faith of Jesus Christ, I am counted as righteous. It is Christ's faith, given to me as a gift, which transforms me from a hopeless sinner to a child of the King. "God saved you by his special favor.... You can't take credit for this; it is a gift from God" (Ephesians 2:8 NLT).

Paul stated this truth again in Galatians 2:20. "...and the life which I now live in the flesh I live by the faith of the Son of God, who loved me and gave Himself for me." The source for faith is never found in human beings. It is never our self-generated "faith" that is at work in our lives, even after we have been given the gift of faith and have been born again.

In Hebrews we learn that Jesus Christ is both the Author (source) and Finisher (continual supplier) of faith (Hebrews 12:2). And faith (Christ's gift of faith to us) comes to us by hearing the Word of God. And unless He gives us ears to hear, faith remains inaccessible to us, even as believers.

The apostle Paul was continually in awe of the miraculous reality of his own salvation. He knew there was no good thing in him that qualified him to be called of God. Rather, he understood that his salvation and his daily walk with the Lord were a result of God's unconditional mercy and grace.

"But God commended His love toward us, in that while we were yet sinners, Christ died for us. Much more...being reconciled, we shall be saved by His life" (Romans 5:8-10). The Lord's righteous life, in addition to His death, counts for us. We are counted as righteous before the Father because Christ lived a perfect life, and we are counting on His work, not ours, day after day. We can then say, with Paul, "Let us give praise to the glory of His grace wherein He (the Father) hath made us accepted in the Beloved (the Son)" (Ephesians 1:6).

And Lord, please give us the grace and the faith to "look unto you" for our fresh supply of faith to face today's circumstances.

Christ and the Holy Spirit...Always Praying for Us

He ever liveth to make intercession for them.
—Hebrews 7:25

Have you ever wondered what the Son discusses with the Father when He talks to Him about you? The Scripture clearly teaches that Jesus Christ "ever lives" to be our Advocate, our Attorney, at the throne of God. That is His purpose as our High Priest, forever and always interceding in our behalf before the Father. He is always discussing with the Father the details that are being worked together for our highest good, individually!

In addition, the Holy Spirit "helps us in our distress. For we don't even know what we should pray for or how we should pray...and the Spirit pleads for us believers in harmony with God's will" (Romans 8:26-27 NLT).

Now here is a question for us to ponder, especially when we are discouraged, distraught, confused, and bewildered: Do we

7

believe that God's perfect will is being worked out in our lives every single minute? The fact that Christ Himself and the Holy Spirit are both continually requesting that the Father's will be done in our lives provides us with the truth of that reality! Their prayers will be answered!

In Hebrews 9:24 we read, "For Christ has entered into heaven itself to appear *now* before God as our Advocate" (emphasis added). The Lord is continually pleading His righteousness in our behalf before the throne of God.

When Satan, our accuser, points out our sins and failures to the Father, Christ, our personal Attorney, speaks to the Father in our defense. Christ is the living proof that He has obtained our eternal redemption. "Once for all time he took blood into that Most Holy Place, but not the blood of goats and calves. He took his own blood, and with it he secured our salvation forever" (Hebrews 9:12 NLT). And again we read, "He came once for all time, at the end of the age, to remove the power of sin forever by his sacrificial death for us" (Hebrews 9:26 NLT).

Do we agree with Satan when he accuses us and itemizes our weakness, sin, and lack of faith, etc., etc.? Or do we agree with the Word of God that we are righteous, forgiven saints, headed for heaven, not because of any good thing in us, but because of Christ's sacrifice and intercession in our behalf? To agree with Satan is to doubt the truth of the Word of God. The accuser of the brethren has one goal and that is to get us to believe lies, just as he did with Eve in the garden. If you and I believe that we are in Christ by His call of grace, we can stand on His Word and dare to rejoice in the truth of the Word about our current condition before the Father.

Who dares accuse us whom God has chosen for His own? Will God? No! He is the one who has given us right standing with himself?.... Who then will condemn us? Will Christ Jesus? No, for he is the one who died for us.... Can anything ever separate us from Christ's love? ...and I am convinced that nothing can ever separate us from his love...Our fears for today, our worries about tomorrow, and even the powers of hell can't keep God's love away.

—Romans 8:33-38 NLT

Oh Lord, help us to not only believe Your Word, but to rest in Your constant love and intercession. Give us eyes to see into the invisible realm of truth rather than looking at this visible realm of deception about who we are. Remind us, by Thy Spirit, how loved and how safe we really are in You.

Sought Out

Thou shall be called, Sought out.
—Isaiah 62:12

The Lord Himself gives the prophet Isaiah the name for His people, those He has redeemed from His wrath. They are to be called "Sought out." Oh, what a huge truth is ours in this passage. And it is a truth that, sadly, we do not often hear from today's teachers and preachers.

God's people are those individuals He Himself sought out among all the billions of human beings on the planet over thousands of years. The Lord told us that He came into the world for one purpose, to seek and to save the lost (Luke 19:10). And if He did not seek us and find us, we would never find Him. We, in our humanity, are at enmity with God. No human being on the planet ever seeks after God unless God reaches out to him or her first (Romans 3:10-11).

But our earthly wisdom argues against this fact. Many even quote the Scriptures which say, "Draw near to God and He will draw near to you" (James 4:8). "Seek the Lord while He may be found" (Isaiah 55:6). "Whosoever comes unto me I will never cast out" (John 6:31).

So what is the answer to these seemingly incompatible truths? The answer comes from the Word itself. In John 6:44 Jesus says, "No man can come to me, except the Father who has sent me draws him." Again Jesus says, "All that the Father gives me shall come to Me and he that comes to Me I will not cast out" (John 6:37).

Clearly, if any person is truly seeking after God, it is because the Holy Spirit has sought him or her out and that person is being drawn by the Spirit, not initially by his or her own human desires.

The next question often raised is "Why does the Bible tell us to seek the Lord or draw near to Him if we can't?" The answer lies in the incredible power inherent in the Word of God. "Faith comes by hearing and hearing by the Word of God" (Romans 10:17). In other words, when an exhortation is given to seek the Lord, the Holy Spirit anoints the ears of those Christ came to save, and we follow Him! The Word of God, the actual written Word, anointed by the Holy Spirit, transforms us. All right behavior or responses that ever flow out of our lives are a result of the Spirit's work in us.

Many of the parables confirm this amazing grace—that the Lord has sought us out. The Shepherd came to seek and to save all of His sheep. He is not willing that any of His sheep perish (Read Matthew 18:11-14). The woman who had ten coins and lost one did the seeking. She brought the light to the coin. The coin did not seek her. Nor do lost sheep seek their shepherd.

The Lord tells us in John 10, "I am the Good Shepherd. I lay down my life for the sheep. My sheep will hear my voice. My sheep will follow me. They will not follow a stranger."

Charles Spurgeon commented on these words of Isaiah, "Thou shalt be called Sought out." He wrote, "The surpassing grace of God is seen very clearly in that we were not only sought, but sought out...we were mingled with the mire... we as lost sheep were desperately lost.... Blessed be His name, He never relinquishes the search until the chosen are sought out effectually...we can find no reason for it but God's own sovereign love...."

This is one of the most life-changing truths in the entire Bible. As Jesus said, "You didn't choose me, I chose you" (John 15:16 NLT).

How recently have we praised Him anew for this incredible display of amazing grace? And this same Shepherd has promised to keep us from all the wild animals of the wilderness and present us faultless and blameless before His throne of grace (Jude 24).

Hallelujah! What a Savior You are, oh Lord!

Seated in Heavenly Realms

For he raised us from the dead along with Christ,
and we are seated with him in the heavenly realms....
—*Ephesians 2:6* NLT

How will we ever grasp what the apostle Paul is telling us here? Only by Spirit revelation! In 1 Corinthians 15:22 we read, "For as in Adam all die...." Because we are related to Adam, the first human being, we are born sinners and are condemned to die. That is a historical, visible, and experiential fact. We don't necessarily understand the how or the why of what happened in the garden of Eden. Yet we are aware that death is a certainty because we are related to Adam. "For the wages of sin is death..." (Romans 6:23). The result of this inheritance is eternal separation from God, Who reigns in heaven.

As mysteriously as condemnation became ours as relatives of Adam, God's amazing grace has provided us with a new inheritance, which was revealed in a different garden. Christ died to pay for the wages of sin and conquered death's power. The empty tomb revealed His identity as God in the flesh. When the Spirit of God opens our eyes to see this truth, we discover that a miracle has occurred. We have been transplanted, out of Adam's heritage and into Christ's heavenly heritage. "If you confess with your mouth that Jesus is Lord and believe in your heart that God raised Him from the dead, you will be saved" (Romans 10:9 NLT).

Not only did God the Father raise Christ from the dead, but we who believe were resurrected with Him! We are already alive eternally, counted as in Christ. We are heavenly beings in the here and now!

What happened to believers at the cross is undeniable. "We were crucified with Him...we died...we were buried with Him" (Romans 6:4-7). What happened to us in His resurrection is equally undeniable, though humanly incomprehensible. "If we died together with Him we...live also with Him" (Romans 6:8). "He raised us up together with Him and made us to sit down together with Him in the heavenly spheres" (Ephesians 2:6).

The apostle Paul continually underscored the miraculous life of those in Christ. "I have been crucified with Christ, yet I live. Yet not I, but Christ liveth in me" (Galatians 2:20). The One who lives in me is reigning in heaven, and I am in Him. "Therefore if any one is in Christ, there is a new creation" (2 Corinthians 5:17). "He rescued us from the power of darkness and translated us into the kingdom of the Son" (Colossians 1:13).

Lord, give us eyes to see and grace to believe who we are in You. Grant us the privilege, by Your mercy, of embracing our heavenly citizenship. Let us live the "above" life here below.

We Have Been Un-Sinned!

Purge me with hyssop and I shall be clean.
—Psalm 51:7

King David wrote Psalm 51 after his adulterous relationship with Bathsheba and after plotting the murder of her husband, Uriah. The entire psalm is a reflection of David's agony over his own sin and failure. And because of that, most of us have a deep appreciation for his agonies and for the comfort he seems to receive from bringing his failures before the Lord.

The New Living Translation reads, "Purify me from my sins and I will be clean." However, the King James Version refers to being purified by the use of "hyssop." Hyssop was a sponge-like plant that the priests of Israel used to spatter the blood of the sacrificial lamb over the entire altar area. This depicted an individual being cleansed from sin, head to toe.

But perhaps even more graphic is the Hebrew meaning behind the word for *purge*. The passage literally reads, "Thou wilt un-sin me and I shall be clean." Think of that! The blood of our Lamb has "un-sinned" us. We are washed clean; we are completely "un-sinned!"

In Isaiah 53:6a we read, "All we like sheep have gone astray; we have turned every one to his own way." As Charles Spurgeon so aptly pointed out, each one of us has his or her own unique set of sins and failures.

David had his; we each have ours—personal failures that are ours alone, proving clearly that we are guilty of specific acts of sin in addition to our basic sin nature. Spurgeon wrote, "There is a peculiar sinfulness about every one of us…all are sinful, but each one with some special aggravation not found in his fellow."

In Isaiah 53:6b we read, "And the Lord hath laid on Him the iniquity of us all." Every one of our "peculiar aggravations" has been laid upon our Lord Jesus. He has un-sinned us from our very own personal acts of sinfulness. All of our sins were future sins when Christ died 2,000 years ago. Yet He knew exactly how each of us would fail over the course of our entire lives. These are the specific past, present, and future individual sins, from which we have been "un-sinned." We have been made as righteous as the Lord Himself, totally un-sinned because of His incredible act of mercy and grace (2 Corinthians 5:29).

The Israelites experienced a visual foreshadowing of this great truth even in the wilderness. On the Day of Atonement, Aaron, the high priest, sacrificed a goat on the altar as a picture of the sin covering of blood. He then took an additional goat—a live goat—and he "lay both of his hands on the goat's head and confessed over it all the sins and rebellion of the Israelites"

(Leviticus 16:21 NLT). Then this scapegoat was led out into the wilderness and released, carrying away all the sins of the people.

Lord, help us clearly see that You are our Scapegoat. We are eternally grateful.

Trust the Lord– Confide in Him

He that trusteth in the Lord, mercy shall compass him about.
—Psalm 32:10

Sometimes, it seems to me that we wonder if we really are "trusting" the Lord. We often feel that "trusting" requires exercising some spiritual muscle we don't feel like we have.

Interestingly, the Hebrew word translated as "trust" in this psalm is *batah*. It occurs in 107 passages in the Old Testament. The root meaning of *batah* is "to confide in." So we could read, "He that confides in the Lord, mercy shall compass him about."

King David was a man after God's own heart. He was deeply loved by the Lord. And David understood what it meant to confide in the Lord. Earlier in Psalm 32 he wrote, "I acknowledged my sin unto thee, and mine iniquity have I not hid. I said 'I will confess my transgressions unto the Lord'"

(Psalm 32:5). Notice that David revealed the result of confiding or confessing his sins to the Lord. Mercy and God's unfailing love encompass one who confides in Him.

Amazingly, mercy and truth are consistently linked in the Scriptures. In Psalm 51, as David agonized over his relationship with Bathsheba, he wrote, "Behold, Thou desirest truth in the inward parts.... Thou desirest not sacrifice" (Psalm 51:6, 16). And David understood the character of the Lord with whom he had a relationship. "According unto the multitude of Thy tender mercies, blot out my transgressions" (Psalm 51:1).

The apostle John is described in the New Testament as the disciple "whom Jesus loved" (John 13:23). He wrote, "If we say that we have no sin we deceive ourselves and the truth is not in us. If we confess our sins, He is faithful and just to forgive us our sins, and to cleanse us from all unrighteousness" (1 John 1:8-9). In other words, it is in telling the truth (confessing) about our sin and failure that our relationship with Christ is both revealed and confirmed. Only His children, those who are alive in Christ, are aware of who they are—sinners who need the Savior every moment.

Walking day by day in Christ is not about exercising our spiritual muscle. Amos, a shepherd and Old Testament prophet, asks this rhetorical question, "Can two walk together except they be agreed?" (Amos 3:3). As believers we agree with the Lord about ourselves and our situation. Even our ability to agree—to confess—is a result of His work in us. He shines the light of His Spirit upon our inward parts, and the truth is revealed to us.

This is the good news. There is no condemnation to those who are in Christ (Romans 8:1). Rather, He speaks peace to His saints, "Mercy and truth are met together; righteousness and peace have kissed each other" (Psalm 85:8-10).

Lord, we rejoice at this miracle of Your love. We confide in You boldly and receive Your tender mercies.

Predestined to be Conformed

*For whom He did foreknow, He also did predestinate
to be conformed to the image of His Son.*
—*Romans 8:29*

Do you sometimes wish you were more loving, generous, patient, or thoughtful? We often chastise ourselves for failing to display the fruit of the Spirit…love, joy, peace, gentleness, patience, etc. And it sometimes seems there is no hope we will ever shape up.

But here is the good news. We will eventually be conformed to the very image of Jesus Christ. We will be as kind, patient, loving, and merciful as He is!

In the New Living Translation we read, "For God knew His people in advance and He chose them to become like His Son…" (Romans 8:29 NLT). Imagine that! He knew how unloving, unkind, and impatient we would be in our humanity. Yet He chose us anyway. He, in His mercy and grace, has promised to make us trophies of His character, on display for the entire universe to behold (Ephesians 2:7).

The apostle Paul promised this same reality to the Philippians. He wrote, "And I am sure that God, who began the good work within you, will continue His work until it is finally finished on that day when Christ Jesus comes back again" (Philippians 1:6 NLT). What a promise! What a future! There is hope—a sure hope—for our becoming as He is.

The prophet Isaiah said what we often feel, "We are not godly. We are constant sinners. How can people like us be saved? We are all infected and impure with sin. When we proudly display our righteous deeds, we find they are but filthy rags.... And yet, Lord, you are our Father. We are the clay and You are the potter. We are all formed by Your hand" (Isaiah 64:5-9 NLT). Isaiah counted on the Lord's mercy and grace. As the Potter and our Father, He will form us into "vessels of honor."

The apostle Paul repeated this same hope. He wrote, "When a potter makes jars of clay...he has the right to pour out the riches of His glory upon those He prepared to be the objects of His mercy—even upon us whom He selected, both from the Jews and from the Gentiles" (Romans 9:21-24 NLT).

The Lord Himself has prayed to God the Father and requested that we might be changed into individuals whose lives will reflect the exact same glory as the life of Christ Himself. "I am praying not only for these disciples but also for all who will ever believe in Me.... I have given them the glory You gave Me, Father...I in them and You in Me, all being perfected into one" (John 17:20-23 NLT).

Perhaps our greatest joy might come from praising the Lord daily that He is faithfully changing us "from glory to glory," transforming us into His own image.

Thank You, Lord, for the faithful work of Your Spirit in us.

Restored from Ruin

He saved us, by the washing of regeneration
and the renewing of the Holy Ghost.
—Titus 3:5

This is one of those verses in the Scripture that can be intimidating with the theological words it contains. Yet the Lord is teaching us some life-changing, transformational realities here. Paul tells us how we were saved. He writes, "by the washing of regeneration and renewing of the Holy Ghost."

What is "the washing of regeneration"? The Greek word for regeneration is *paliggenesis*. It refers to a spiritual rebirth and, literally, means a "spiritual renovation." It relates to another Greek word, *apokatasis* or restitution, a reestablishment from a state of ruin! In other words, God has created a complete renovation work in us. We have been taken from "ruin" to righteousness, miraculously.

Christ spoke of this process when He told Nicodemus, "Unless you are born again, you can never see the kingdom of God…no one can enter the kingdom of God without being born of water and the Spirit…the Holy Spirit gives new life from heaven" (John 3:3, 5, 7 NLT).

Notice that Paul refers to the "washing" of regeneration and Jesus refers to being born of "water." This is one of the great mysteries in God's working in us. In Ephesians 5:26 we read that the Lord sanctifies and cleanses us by "the washing of water by the word." The Word of God is the agent that regenerates us. It washes and cleanses. It has miraculous power.

In Romans 10:17 we read, "Faith comes by hearing, and hearing by the Word of God." Our regeneration, being restored from ruin, happened when we heard and believed the Word of God. Paul says that he is "not ashamed of the gospel of Christ for it is the power of God unto salvation…." Our ability to even hear and believe is a result of the Lord opening our ears. Not everyone who simply hears the gospel becomes regenerated. But when He gives us faith to believe the Word, we are washed by it, regenerated. This process, this work, is miraculous. Jesus said, "You can't explain how people are born of the Spirit" (John 3:8 NLT). The process itself is beyond our understanding ultimately.

In the Titus passage, we also read that we are saved by "the renewing of the Holy Ghost." The Greek word for renewing is *anakainosis*, which refers to the ongoing restorative work which occurs in us as believers. We are regenerated by the Word—we are brought back from ruin. Then the Holy Spirit continues that ongoing work by renewing our mind (Romans 12:2) and increasing our knowledge and understanding of what this miraculous life in Christ really is (Colossians 3:10).

There is miraculous, restorative power in Your Word, Lord. Open our ears and our hearts that we might be renewed in You. Thank You for restoring us from the ruin we once were.

Kindness

Our lives were full of evil and envy...
but then God our Savior showed us His kindness and love.
—Titus 3:3-4 NLT

It seems like kindness is an almost forgotten word in our world today. What images come to your mind when you think of the word *kindness*? Isn't it true that we long to have others show kindness to us, to be tender and forgiving toward us? Isn't it a blessing in our lives when others don't condemn us for our failures, our inadequacies, and our weaknesses?

In the Scripture the word *kindness* is almost always connected with the word *show*. For example, consider the following verses:

> Show kindness, I pray thee, unto me, and make mention of me unto Pharaoh.
>
> —Genesis 40:14

Now therefore, I pray you…since I have showed you kindness, that ye will also show kindness unto my father's house.

—Joshua 2:12

Blessed be thou of the Lord…for thou hast showed more kindness.

—Ruth 3:10

The people of the island were very kind to us. It was cold and rainy, so they built a fire on the shore to welcome us and warm us.

—Acts 28:2 NLT

Aren't those great words, to be "welcomed" and "warmed"? That is what the Lord is to us. He is always welcoming us into His presence, showering us with the warmth of His love, displaying kindness. No condemnation. Never even remembering our sins (Isaiah 43:25).

In the Hebrew language the word for kindness is *chesed*. This is the same word, *chesed*, that is translated as *mercy* in the Old Testament. In Psalm 103:17 we read, "The mercy of the Lord is from everlasting to everlasting." In Isaiah 54:8 the prophet writes, "With everlasting kindness will I have mercy on thee saith the Lord thy Redeemer." The Lord's kindness toward us is unchanging, stretching from eternity past into the eternal future.

In the New Testament one of the Greek words for kindness is *chrestotes*. Paul wrote, "God…has raised us up…in Christ Jesus that in the ages to come He might show the exceeding riches of His grace in His kindness toward us through Christ Jesus"

(Ephesians 2:4-7 NLT). The Lord will forever be displaying His kindness toward us!

Perhaps one of the greatest gifts we can give others is to show kindness to them…day after day. When the Holy Spirit reveals to us the kindness God the Savior has shown us, we are given the grace to shower that kindness on others. The apostle Peter wrote, "Continue to show deep love for each other, for love covers a multitude of sins…" (1 Peter 4:8 NLT). What a wonderful reminder that we should love one another with a kindness that overlooks sin and failure, even as He has "overlooked" our own sins and failures.

David, the psalmist, prayed, "Deal with thy servant according unto thy mercy…" (Psalm 119:124). The word for mercy, again, is *chesed*. "Deal with me according to thy loving kindness…" David was saying, "Please, Lord, don't deal with me according to what I deserve!"

Lord, may we pour out the warm, welcoming kindness of Your heart on others.

The Celebration of Freedom

Ye shall know the truth and the truth shall set you free.
—John 8:32

As Americans, we celebrate our independence—our freedom as a country. We became free from foreign rulership. And our freedom is something we treasure. In fact, we attempt to bring freedom to countries enslaved by wicked, corrupt rulers. We do so because we have experienced the incredible blessings inherent in our freedom as citizens of the United States of America.

The Bible describes the entire human race as being enslaved, ruled by the ravages of sin. The apostle Paul described those who are not in Christ as "slaves to sin," the end result being death eternally (Romans 6:17, 22). He then explained that the gift of God to believers is having been set free from this enslavement through faith in Jesus Christ.

The Lord Himself describes for us how this happens. "Ye shall know the truth and the truth shall set you free." The Greek word for truth is *alethia* and it actually means reality. You will know the reality and in knowing that reality, you will be set free from the ravages of sin.

What is "the reality?" The Lord tells us clearly. "I am the way, the truth and the life. No man comes unto the Father except by Me" (John 14:6). Jesus says, "I am reality." Isn't it interesting that truth is counted as relative in most philosophical discussions today? Yet the Lord says He is the truth, the only absolute reality.

And Christ says we are set free when we know the truth—when we know Him—for He is the truth. The Greek word for knowing in John 8:32 is *ginosko,* which means "to become thoroughly acquainted with," to recognize Christ for Who He is. Thomas still had his doubts after the crucifixion. But once he touched the Lord's scars and spoke to Him in His resurrected body, Thomas recognized Who He was. "My Lord and My God" (John 20:28). Philip was expressing confusion about his own grasp of Who Christ really was and Jesus explained to him, "He that has seen Me has seen the Father" (John 14:9).

Sometimes we fail to recognize or appreciate the hopeless condition we were in before Christ became known to us. Paul said we were held in captivity by sin (Romans 7:23). The word *captivity* actually means to have been taken prisoner at the point of a spear or held in chains. Paul then said that Christ rose from the dead and led "a group of captives out of their captivity" and into the safety and freedom of Himself (Ephesians 4:8).

Individuals who live in a nation controlled by wicked rulers often live in fear for their very lives. There is a constant sense of unrest, not knowing what terrible event might unfold next. Usually there are restrictions of every kind in terms of personal activities or freedom of expression. There is very little, if any, peace and joy for those who live in those conditions. To be set free from that kind of a situation must be an incredible gift.

The Scripture says that Satan is the ruler, the "god of this world" in which we live (2 Corinthians 4:4). We are held captive by him until the Savior becomes known to us. And when He comes and sets us free from our hopeless condition, we enter into an entirely new realm. We have a new Ruler Who overflows with love, mercy, and grace. He is the great Giver of gifts. We can now dare to live in peace, knowing we are safe and secure, free from anxiety and worry about our future. And this Savior has promised to supply all our present needs as well. "Ask and it shall be given unto you" (Matthew 7:7). No wonder we want to share this freedom with others!

The apostle Paul experienced being taken prisoner many times. Yet he rejoiced even while in jail because he knew the truth. He wrote, "God has not given us a spirit of fear; but of power, and of love, and of a sound mind" (2 Timothy 1:7).

Oh Lord, give us the grace to appreciate what it really means to have been "set free" by Your death and resurrection that conquered Satan's hold on us. May we live in that freedom, without fear or anxiety, no matter what our circumstances may be. You are a gracious King.

The Gift of Repentance

Joy shall be in heaven over one sinner that repents.
—Luke 15:7

Repentance does not seem to be a popular word. We often think that "to repent" means to grovel on our knees and beg for forgiveness of sin. Well, that could well be the result of some serious repentance. But the Greek word for repentance is *metanoia*, and it means "a change of mind." To repent is to completely change your mind or your viewpoint about a person, a situation, or yourself—to see things differently.

The parable of the prodigal son in Luke 15 is an example of repentance in action. We read that this young man took his inheritance, left his father, and went "into a far country, and there wasted his substance on riotous living" (Luke 15:13). A series of circumstances then unfolded in his life. No money, no food, and a famine set in. No one was willing to help him.

Suddenly this young man decided to return to his father and ask for forgiveness. The prodigal son experienced a radical change of mind. That is precisely how conversion is experienced—a radical change of mind occurs.

The question is this: When a person repents and becomes a believer in Jesus Christ as God in the flesh, as Savior, what causes the mind to change?

Initially we might say that getting better information, getting new knowledge, discovering the facts about Christ will produce repentance. That may happen, but the cause for true change is not the result of the thinking process. Paul told us that the person who is not a believer can't understand thoughts about the Lord (1 Corinthians 2:14). An unbeliever cannot "think" himself or herself into believing. Again, what produces a change of mind?

In writing to young Timothy, Paul encouraged him to study the Word and avoid foolish arguments over theology. Then he told Timothy to patiently, gently instruct people in the Word of God, "in the hope that God will grant them repentance leading them to a knowledge of the truth" (2 Timothy 2:25 NIV). Repentance is a gift from God. And when He gives us this change of mind, we are led to a knowledge of the truth!

The disciples understood clearly that repentance (coming to believe that Christ is Savior) is totally the work of God's Holy Spirit in a life. In the case of Cornelius, the Gentile Roman soldier to whom Jewish Peter was called to preach the gospel, we see this fact clearly. As Peter preached to the Gentiles, the Holy Spirit "fell on all of them which heard the word" (Acts 10:44). When Peter recounted this event to the Jewish disciples in Jerusalem, they responded with, "Then has God also to the

Gentiles granted repentance" which leads to eternal life (Acts 11:18).

Paul wrote in Romans 2:4 that it is God's goodness and kindness that lead us to repentance. Peter, preaching in the book of Acts, said Christ has been exalted as Savior "to give repentance to Israel, and forgiveness of sins" (Acts 5:31).

It is also fascinating to note that in the parables of the lost sheep, the lost coin, and the lost (prodigal) son, "being found" is identified as repentance. When the shepherd finds his lost sheep, this produces "joy in heaven over one sinner that repents" (Luke 15:7). When the woman finds her lost coin, there is "joy in the presence of the angels of God over one sinner that repents" (Luke 15:10). And the father says of his repentant son, "This thy brother…was lost and is found" (Luke 15:32). Repentance is the result of the good Shepherd seeking us out. Repentance is the result of having been found and saved by the Savior. It is the evidence of our salvation. Repentance, therefore, is not something we do that gets God to respond. Repentance is what we do as a result of His shedding light in our hearts.

If the angels are that thrilled over one sinner repenting, perhaps we need to rejoice anew over the gift of repentance. The Lord did not come to save good people; He came to find lost sinners and lead them to Himself. Rejoice if you know you have been found! And those of us who have been found have at least one thing in common: We know we are sinners because His light shone into our hearts and we saw our "lostness" apart from Him.

Oh Lord, send us each day into the world to gather Your lost sheep through the drawing power of Your Spirit.

The One and Only Faith

*Contend for the faith which was once
delivered unto the saints.*
—Jude 3

The Greek word for faith, when used as a noun, is *pistis*. And often in the Scripture the article *the* appears before the noun. "Contend for the faith." Paul talks about "the faith of Abraham" (Romans 4:16); He wants us to be "established in the faith" (Colossians 2:7). He says, "Examine yourselves, whether you be in the faith" (2 Corinthians 13:5); and some have "erred from the faith" (1 Timothy 6:10). So what exactly is the faith that has been delivered to the saints?

The apostle Paul used some specific language about the faith in Galatians 2:16. In the King James Version we read, "A man is not justified by the works of the law, but by the faith of Jesus Christ, even we have believed in Jesus Christ, that we might be justified by the faith of Christ." And in Galatians 2:20 we read,

36

"Christ lives in me, and the life which I now live in the flesh I live by the faith of the Son of God, who loved me and gave Himself for me."

Notice how many references highlight "the faith of Jesus Christ." Most newer translations change the "of" to "in" faith in Jesus Christ. Yet, let's examine the true Source of faith. In Hebrews 12:2 we are told to live the Christian life by "...looking unto Jesus the Author and Finisher of faith." Jesus Christ is the sole Source of the faith described by all the biblical writers.

In the Jude 3 passage we read that "the faith has been delivered" to us. Who delivered the faith to the saints? The Greek word for delivered is *paradidomi*. In 1 Corinthians 15:3-5 Paul describes what he delivered (*paradidomi*) to the saints. Notice that Paul said he delivered that which he received. Who delivered the life-changing truth to Paul? Christ Himself brought the faith to Paul on the road to Damascus. He revealed Himself as Lord, the One Who has conquered sin and death.

Paul went on to tell us what was delivered to him. "How that Christ died for our sins...that He was buried, and that He rose again the third day" (1 Corinthians 15:4). This, the gospel, is the faith that saves us. And in Ephesians we learn that it is God's grace that saves us through the means of faith, which is a gift (Ephesians 2:8-9). The faith has been delivered to the saints as a gift.

Paul said he was sent as an apostle of Jesus Christ to further the faith of God's elect and their knowledge of the truth (Titus 1:1).

Why is this issue of the faith so important? First, today's culture abounds in "spirituality" talk. Many people talk about having faith. They tell others to have faith and write books encouraging the exercising of faith. Individuals say, "I have faith in the outworking of the universe." None of this reflects the biblical definition of faith. The faith described in the Bible is the belief, the reality, the truth that Christ died for our sins and rose from the dead to prove He alone is Lord over all.

Second, we need to understand that the faith we have has been delivered to us; it is a gift. It is the faith of Jesus Christ, our Deliverer, Who takes away our sins (Romans 11:26-27). The life of Christ in every believer is a result of His giving us the faith. And in our daily lives we are "kept by the power of God through faith unto salvation, ready to be revealed in the last time" (1 Peter 1:5). His power sustains us by the gift of faith.

Finally, it is sobering to read that "without faith it is impossible to please God" (Hebrews 11:6). No amount of good behavior or believing in the mysterious work of "the universe" will count with God. "Whatsoever is not of faith is sin" (Romans 14:23). In other words, every action that springs from any other source than the Faith-Source, Jesus Christ, is counted as sin—even if the world views an action as "good."

May we be "found in Him, not having our own righteousness, which is of the law, but that which is through the faith of Christ, the righteousness which is of God, by faith" (Philippians 3:9).

The God of All Grace

But the God of all grace who hath called us unto
His eternal glory by Christ Jesus,
after that ye have suffered a while, make you perfect,
establish, strengthen, settle you!
—*1 Peter 5:10*

If anyone was qualified to talk about the grace of God it would be Peter. Imagine the personal agony he carried his entire life when he remembered his denial of the Lord on the very eve of Christ's greatest suffering. In Christ's greatest hour of need, Peter was not there for Him, the One with Whom Peter had spent virtually every day and night for three full years.

Have you ever looked back on past failures in your life and agonized over them? There is no place to go with that pain—except to "the God of all grace." He isn't the God of "a little" grace. His entire being is the God of grace. He is all grace! In his darkest hour, the prophet Jonah knew the character of God. "I know that Thou art a gracious God, and merciful, slow to anger, and of great kindness…" (Jonah 4:2).

David knew God as the God of all grace in his darkest hour. "Have mercy upon me, O God, according to Thy loving kindness (Hebrew word for grace) (Psalm 51:1).

Through his own failure, the apostle Paul had experienced God's character. He described the Lord as "the God of patience and consolation (comfort)" (Romans 15:5). Paul went on to describe Him as "the God of hope" Who fills us with joy and peace so that we can "abound in hope" (Romans 15:13).

Stephen, the martyr who was stoned to death, described the Lord as "the God of glory" (Acts 7:2). Peter said that the God of all grace has "called us unto His eternal glory." Peter, like Stephen, knew Him as the God of glory. Peter had actually seen the Lord in His glory at the Mount of Transfiguration.

In 1 Peter 5:1 we learn that, even though this earthly life includes suffering, we will ultimately be "made perfect." (The Greek word for perfect is *katartizo* and means to "be arranged or set in order.") In addition, Peter said that the God of all grace will "establish, strengthen, and settle" us. We will be secure, on a firm foundation.

And the apostle Paul described the Lord as "the God of love and peace" (2 Corinthians 13:11). Surely Peter must have only found inner peace *after* he experienced the Lord's love, *after* the resurrection. Following His resurrection, Christ spoke with Peter one on one, calling him by name. He encouraged Peter to confess his love for Him three times, and then Christ commissioned Peter to be a leader among the saints. Our peace in the Lord follows after our knowledge of being fully loved and forgiven by Him.

What a Savior, the God of all grace, Who never abandons us, even in our failures! He is, for each of us, the God of glory, the God of hope, the God of patience, the God of comfort, the God of love, and the God of peace. May He be to you whichever one of those you most need right now.

Father, thank You for Your very essence! Thank You for being full of infinite grace.

Sufficient Grace

My grace is sufficient for thee.
—2 Corinthians 12:9

The marvelous old hymn written in the early 1900s, "Wonderful Grace of Jesus," is rich with biblical truth.

> Wonderful grace of Jesus, Greater than all my sin. How shall my tongue describe it? Where shall its praise begin? Taking away my burden, setting my spirit free. For the wonderful grace of Jesus reaches me.
>
> —Haldor Lillenas

The first time the word *grace* appears in the Bible is in Genesis 6:8. "Noah found grace in the eyes of the Lord." The Hebrew word is *chen* which means favor. God looked upon Noah with favor. Repeatedly in the Old Testament, the grace of God is connected with God's look, His eyes, what He sees.

"And the Lord said unto Moses, 'I will do this thing that thou hast spoken; for thou has found grace in My sight, and I know thee by name'" (Exodus 33:17).

Do you ever question whether or not God looks upon you with favor? Do you wonder if, when His eyes rest upon you, those eyes are full of grace toward you? The apostle Paul wrestled with this issue when he was under satanic attack. He begged the Lord to deliver him from his circumstances. The Lord's response was, "My gracious favor is all you need. My power works best in your weakness" (2 Corinthians 12:9 NLT).

In the book of Romans Paul reminds us of the basis upon which we can be participants in God's grace, His favor. "We have peace with God through our Lord Jesus Christ: By whom also we have access by faith into this grace wherein we stand..." (Romans 5:1-2). The only basis for us to be looked upon by grace is "through our Lord Jesus Christ." Through Christ's death on the cross, we experience cleansing from all sin as we place our faith in this reality...that Christ shed His blood for you, for me, personally.

In Romans 5 Paul goes on to say, "When we were utterly helpless, Christ came at just the right time and died for us sinners.... And since we have been made right in God's sight by the blood of Christ, we have been restored to friendship with God" (Romans 5:6-10 NLT).

Think of those words, "utterly helpless." Aren't there times (maybe even at this moment) that we feel "utterly helpless" to get our lives together spiritually? We are "without strength;" we may be full of self-condemnation, self-loathing. Or we may simply feel empty, with no sense of the Lord's purpose or grace in our lives.

It is in these very circumstances that the Word of God comes to us, His Word—the only living truth in the universe. And He says to you, to me, as He said to Moses, "I will do this thing… for you have found grace in My sight, and I know you by name" (Exodus 33:17).

The Lord called us to Himself. He called us by name. "He calls his own sheep by name and leads them out" (John 10:3). While we were still sinners, unconscious of the Person of Jesus Christ, He died for us. He paid for our sins, all of them. "While we were yet sinners, Christ died for us" (Romans 5:8). And now He is looking upon us with favor, working all things (everything in our current circumstances) together for our highest good. "Oh, the wonderful grace of Jesus, greater than all my sin."

Charles Spurgeon wrote, "God's grace is illustrated and magnified in the poverty and trials of believers. Saints bear up under every discouragement, believing that all things work together for their good, and out of apparent evils a real blessing shall ultimately spring…."

Lord, give us grace to believe that Your "wonderful grace reaches even me."

Grace is Being Brought to You

Wherefore, gird up the loins of your mind, be sober,
and hope to the end for the grace that is to be brought
unto you at the revelation of Jesus Christ.
—1 Peter 1:13

Imagine that! Grace is being brought to us. When the Lord returns, when the unveiling of Jesus Christ occurs, some amazing gifts will be brought to us. And Peter suggested that we set our hope in this life squarely on what is coming to us.

In Romans 8:18 Paul wrote "that the sufferings of this present time are not worthy to be compared with the glory which shall be revealed in us." Not only is grace being brought to us, glory is also being brought to us when Christ is unveiled!

Peter elaborated on additional blessings coming to us when Christ is revealed to the world. He said "there is a wonderful joy" coming as well and we are to be glad about that even now. (1 Peter 1:6 NLT). And he said we are going to receive the fullness, the completeness, of our salvation. We will be, experientially, eternally alive (1 Peter 1:5). The apostle Paul also described that experience. He wrote that when Christ comes we will have "strong hearts," we will be fully "blameless" and completely "holy" (1 Thessalonians 2:13 NLT). What a future is promised, ordained, and designed for us as believers!

Another awesome aspect of our future is this: Christ is bringing us a new body. "For when the trumpet sounds, the Christians who have died will be raised with transformed bodies. And then we who are living will be transformed so that we will never die" (1 Corinthians 15:52 NLT).

The apostle John talked about additional incredible gifts that will be brought to believers at the unveiling of Christ before the world. The Lord will bring us each "a new name that no one knows except the one who receives it" (Revelation 2:17 NLT). And we will discover a "new song," which we will sing in unison with "every creature in heaven and on earth and under the earth and in the sea" (Revelation 5:9, 13 NLT).

Finally, we "will see his face, and his name will be written" on our foreheads. And we will "reign" with Him forever and ever (Revelation 22:4 NLT). May we "gird up the loins of our mind" and set our hope on the future that is ours, given to us already, and being personally delivered to us by the King Who is coming!

Lord, what an incredible reality! You will bring us grace and unending abundance. What love, Lord!

Manifold Mercies

*By his great mercy, we have been born anew to a living hope
through the resurrection of Jesus Christ from the dead.*
—*1 Peter 1:3 RSV*

In both the Old and New Testaments the very nature of our Lord
is described as being full of mercy. Both the Hebrew word and
the Greek word for mercy mean loving-kindness. The saints of
old knew the very heart of the Creator. The prophet Jonah said,
"For I knew that Thou art a gracious God, and merciful, slow
to anger, and of great kindness…" (Jonah 4:2).

The apostle Peter personally experienced the "great mercy"
of the Lord as Christ called Peter to carry the gospel even after
Peter had denied the Lord three times. Peter was a recipient of
the Lord's lovingkindness. He writes, "All honor to the God
and Father of our Lord Jesus Christ, for it is by his boundless
mercy that God has given us the privilege of being born again"
(1 Peter 1:3 NLT).

In the King James Version this verse reads "abundant mercy." The Greek word for abundant or boundless is derived from the word *polus,* which is often translated *manifold.* The definition of manifold includes multiplied by many thousands.

Have we even begun to comprehend that, if we know Jesus Christ personally, having been born again, it is because of His boundless, manifold mercy toward us? Think of what that says about us before the Lord revealed Himself to us. What condition were we in that required "mercy multiplied by the myriad of ten thousand?"

The apostle Paul answered that question for us again and again. He said, "You were a slave to sin," held captive by the "mighty powers of darkness," a sinner on the path to destruction (Romans 6:17; Ephesians 6:12; Romans 6:23).

Somehow most of us have never really viewed ourselves in that serious a condition. Would you agree? Yet the Lord describes us as in that condition because that is how far removed we were (as human beings outside of Christ) from the glorious perfection of God Himself.

Paul went on to say that the Lord Himself has to rescue us from our condition because we are blind to our own condition. "Once you were dead, doomed forever.... But God is so rich in mercy, and He loved us so very much that...He gave us life when He raised Christ from the dead. It is only by God's special favor that you have been saved" (Ephesians 2:1, 4-5 NLT).

It might be good to pause here and lift up our hearts to praise Him for His "manifold mercy" to us personally. Perhaps it would be good to agree with Him afresh that we need all the mercy He pours out on us—every moment of every day.

The prophet Jeremiah experienced insurmountable pain and suffering as he saw the waywardness of his people, the

Israelites. He was persecuted and mistreated. In the midst of this condition he penned the truth of Who he knew the Lord to be. "The unfailing love of the Lord never ends! By His mercies we have been kept from complete destruction. Great is His faithfulness; His mercies begin afresh each day" (Lamentations 3:22-23 NLT).

Are we counting on His "unfailing love" and His "manifold mercies" in our specific circumstances today? Do we actually believe that everything unfolding in our lives is flowing from His lovingkindness toward us? How would our mindset change today if we embraced this reality?

What if we consciously placed our every concern, from our tiniest disturbance in life to our major worry or unhappiness, in His hands? Suppose we were to embrace the omnipotence of the One Whose love never fails and Whose endless mercy is being poured unto our hearts and lives this very moment. Perhaps we could then sing again the words of the famous old hymn written by William Newell in 1895, entitled "At Calvary."

Years I spent in vanity and pride.
Caring not my Lord was crucified.
Knowing not it was for me He died on Calvary.
Mercy there was great and grace was free.
Pardon there was multiplied to me.
There my burdened soul found liberty, at Calvary.

Lord, may we rest in Your mercy today. May we embrace the liberating reality that Your mercy in salvation extends to us right where we are, here and now.

Peculiar Reasons

Therefore will the Lord wait that
He may be gracious unto you.
—Isaiah 30:18

Charles Spurgeon commented on this verse, "Our Father has reasons peculiar to Himself for thus keeping us waiting." In our world of "instant everything," waiting is one of our most difficult assignments as believers.

We want to know now if our teenager has been admitted to the college we prefer; we want to know now if we should quit our job and move or if we should go back to college or if we should sell our house. In this material world we are mostly preoccupied with the visible, tangible, concrete issues of living. And these issues are of prime importance to us. Our emotions rise and fall based on the outcomes. We get discouraged and depressed if no answer is in sight.

Yet the prophet Isaiah told us that what is unfolding in the invisible world of the Spirit is what is truly important. The Lord is actively at work, waiting. Why is He waiting to answer our requests or change our circumstances? He is waiting so "that He may be gracious" to us. He wants to "show you favor" or "grace" to us. Spurgeon said He tarries so that "He may the more fully display the riches of His grace" to us.

Don't you wonder what John the Baptist thought about the Lord's "waiting" to rescue him? John never saw "the riches of His grace" in this world. Instead he was beheaded. Here was the man about whom the Lord said, "Verily I say unto you, among them that are born of women there has not arisen anyone greater than John the Baptist" (Matthew 11:11).

Yet John the Baptist experienced confusion and loss of hope. He sent two of his own disciples to ask if Jesus really was the Messiah (Luke 7:18-23). Remember also that John the Baptist and Jesus were second cousins and had grown up together as family. Today as John the Baptist lives in the presence of the Lord, he understands the grace and glory of why the Lord waited.

Like John the Baptist, we may not see the visible answers to some of our agonies this side of heaven. Yet with Job we learn to say, "Though He slay me, I will trust Him" (Job 13:15). Job was sustained by his faith in the invisible work of God. Job had his heart and life set on the heavenlies. "For I know that my Redeemer liveth, and that He shall stand at the latter day upon the earth. And though worms destroy this body, yet in my flesh I shall see God" (Job 19:25- 26).

One of the most magnificent displays of the wisdom of God in waiting is seen in Lazarus' life. In John chapter eleven we are told that Jesus' good friend Lazarus was sick. His sisters, Mary and Martha, whom Jesus also dearly loved (John 11:5), sent a message to Jesus letting Him know of this serious situation.

When Jesus heard this, He explained to His disciples that Lazarus would not die and that his illness was designed to glorify the Son of God and bring glory to God the Father. And He stayed where He was for two more days!

Meanwhile, Mary and Martha were frantic and Lazarus died. Jesus knew Lazarus had died, and He said to the disciples, "I am glad for your sakes I was not there." Jesus was glad He wasn't there to cure Lazarus' sickness!

By the time Jesus and the disciples arrived in Bethany, Lazarus' hometown, Lazarus had been dead four days. And both Martha and Mary cried, saying, "If You had been here Lazarus wouldn't have died." They were essentially blaming the Lord for waiting too long before coming. They had asked Him to come while there was still hope. They were all good friends. They knew Jesus loved them. Why didn't He come? Haven't we had some of those questions when a loved one dies or a newborn dies or an "accident" happens?

We know the rest of the story with Lazarus. The Lord raised Lazarus from the dead and "then many of the Jews which came to Mary and had seen the things which Jesus did, believed on Him" (John 11:45).

Because Lazarus died, there are many in heaven. They believed because they witnessed his resurrection. And imagine the personal testimony Lazarus had. He had visited heaven and returned to earth. What glory God must have received as Lazarus described from firsthand experience the wonders of heaven!

Lord, may we not despair in the waiting, but rather rest in Your coming glory and grace. May we trust Your "peculiar reasons" for all You are doing or not doing in our lives.

Sanctification

*Now may the God of peace make you holy in
every way, and may your whole spirit and soul
and body be kept blameless until that day when
our Lord Jesus Christ comes again. God, who
calls you, is faithful; he will do this.*
—*1 Thessalonians 5:23-24* NLT

Heavenly Rewards and Earthly Works

For the Son of man shall come in the glory of his
Father with his angels; and then he shall
reward every man according to his works.
—Matthew 16:27

These words, and others with a similar ring, are often the greatest joy stealers in our Christian lives. We hear or read the phrase, "according to his works," and instantly our own inadequacy and failures rise up to condemn us.

Stop right there for a moment. Who is the "accuser of the brethren?" The enemy is the one who comes in to tell us we have not "measured up" to God's highest expectations. Yet we read, "If God be for us, who can be against us?...Who shall lay anything to the charge of God's elect?...Nay, in all these things we are more than conquerors through Him that loved us" (Romans 8:31, 33, 37).

What is Christ telling us in Matthew 16:27? For what works will we be rewarded? Jesus Himself answers this question in John 6:28-29. The multitude recognized Jesus as a great teacher sent by God. They did not understand that He was God in the flesh. These people wanted to "work" their way into God's grace. They asked, "What shall we do, that we might work the works of God?" (John 6:28).

Stop right there once again. Isn't that our cry? "What shall I do, Lord, to work the works that will please You?" Before we look at Jesus' answer, what is your answer to that question?

"Jesus answered and said unto them, 'This is the work of God, that ye believe on him whom he hath sent.'" That is the Lord's answer. Believe. The Greek word is *pisteuo,* which means "to have faith."

So the answer is: to do the work of God is to have faith in His Son. How do we do that? Humanly, we cannot work the works of God. Faith is a gift. The Lord Himself supplies faith to those whom He has called. "For by grace are you saved through faith; and that not of yourselves, it is the gift of God. Not of works lest any man should boast" (Ephesians 2:8-9).

Stop once more. Here is where confusion grips us. We can believe that salvation is a gift, but often we are taught that now that our sins are removed, we are responsible for our rewards. We are often told that there is something we can do. We can contribute to our heavenly rewards. This is simply not true. Let's examine what the Word of God says.

In Ephesians 2:10 we read, "For we are his workmanship, created in Christ Jesus unto good works, which God hath before ordained that we should walk in them." God has already ordained our purpose if we are His children in Christ. We will accomplish the works for which we will be rewarded. In 1 Peter 1:4 we are told that the Father is bringing us, by the resurrection of Christ from the dead, into an inheritance that is incorruptible, reserved in heaven for each of us individually.

The Christians in Galatia became "works"-oriented after coming to Christ. Paul wrote to them and said, "Oh, foolish Galatians…did you receive the Spirit by faith or by good deeds.…Having begun in the Spirit, are you now trying to be perfect by self-effort?" (Galatians 3:1-3 Author paraphrase).

Much more can be said on this topic. Theologians argue about our need to be "responsible laborers" in the service of the King. Yet the mystery lies in the fact that without Christ we can do nothing. Therefore, we are to look to Him by faith, believing that He will accomplish His work in us (Philippians 1:6).

The alternative is to look to our own wisdom to ascertain what works we should do and to depend on our own commitment or ability to do them. This leads to pride when we are successful in doing good works. Or it leads to constant pressure—self-inflicted—to try to accomplish enough good works to get more rewards. Or it leads to despair at our lack of good works.

When Jesus hands out rewards for service, the recipients, we discover, are actually unaware that they have done a good work! They ask, "When did we do these things for which you are rewarding us?" (Read Matthew 25:34-40.)

Count on Him. "For it is God who works in you, both to will and to do of His good pleasure" (Philippians 2:13).

Father, thank You for ordaining the works that are ours alone and for safely keeping the inheritance You have ordained for us.

What it Means to be Holy

Follow peace with all men, and holiness
without which no man shall see the Lord.
—Hebrews 12:14

Would you be willing to call yourself "holy?" If you know Who Jesus Christ is, the Scripture says you are holy. And the Bible clearly states, "Without holiness...no man [or woman!] shall see the Lord."

Do we really understand what it means to be holy? It does not mean "being good" or "living a pure life" or "giving money to the poor," etc. These actions do not make us holy.

In fact, Jesus had some very strong words against some very religious people who considered themselves to be holy. The Jewish religious leaders kept the law scrupulously. They prayed several times a day. They gave money to the temple. They attended synagogue often.

Jesus said to these, "How terrible it will be for you teachers of religious law and you Pharisees. Hypocrites! You are like whitewashed tombs—beautiful on the outside but filled on the inside with dead people's bones and all sorts of impurity. You try to look like upright people outwardly, but inside your hearts are filled with hypocrisy and lawlessness" (Matthew 23:27-28 NLT).

You will notice that Jesus indicates that these people may be doing good works, performing well. However, His concern is with their hearts. Think about this for a moment. Can you make your heart holy?

Most people today think that God grades on a curve. Therefore, if we can perform better than the worst scoundrels, we think we will probably make it to heaven. But the Lord does not look on outward appearances. Instead He says, "God blesses those whose hearts are pure, for they will see God."

Holiness demands that we be pure from the inside out. And no human being is! This is why the Lord says, "Unless you are born again, you can never see the kingdom of God" (John 3:3 NLT). The Lord Himself must open our eyes to see that Christ alone is holy. He alone is pure. He must give us His holiness. And that is what happens when we are made holy! The Greek word for holy is *hagios*. It has nothing to do with performance or good works. It means to be set apart by God to be His very own. That requires the miracle of the new birth, being born again. Only the Spirit of God can create a new heart in us. (Read John 3:1-18.)

All who believe that Jesus Christ is God and believe that He died for our sins, personally, are counted as holy, set apart for heaven. Our outward actions may not always reflect the fact that we are counted as holy; but neither will our outward actions contribute to our holiness.

We can rest in His grace and His life. God is the only source of holiness. "I am the Lord, who makes you holy" (Exodus 31:13 NLT). He will faithfully work, by the power of the Holy Spirit, to conform us to His image. The result is a life that does indeed reflect good works and a deep desire to please Him, to be obedient. However, this result flows from God at work in us, willing and doing His good pleasure.

Thank You, oh, Lord, that You are holy and You have stamped us with Your holiness.

Saved by His Life

For if, when we were enemies, we were reconciled to
God by the death of His Son, much more being reconciled,
we shall be saved by His life.
—Romans 5:10

Let's look afresh at what this truth from the Word of God tells us. While we were enemies of God, literally God-haters, we were reconciled to Him, to God. The word reconciled, in the Greek, is *katalasso,* which means to be "restored to divine favor," to be friends once again.

While we were still hating Him, God devised a plan, which He enacted. He sovereignly arranged for us to be His friends. This reconciliation was brought about "by the death of His Son." Jesus announced in John 10 that He was going to the cross to die for the sins of the sheep. "The good shepherd giveth his life for the sheep.... I lay down my life for the sheep" (John 10:11,15). The wages, or price tag, of sin is death. Jesus paid the debt for us. And He did this for us before we were even born into the world. In fact, He chose us to be His own before the foundation of the world. "For God made Christ, who never sinned, to be the offering for our sin, so that we could be made right with God through Christ" (2 Corinthians 5:21 NLT).

In Revelation 13:8 we read that "the Lamb was slain from the foundation of the world." Adam's sin in the garden was no surprise to the Father. He knew that His sheep would enter into the world in a lost condition because of Adam's sin. He sent His Son to seek and to save the lost sheep, to return us to our home with Him in heaven (1 Peter 2:25).

Look again at the Romans 5:10 text. Paul said something even more amazing. "Much more, being reconciled, we shall be saved by His life." Not only did the Lord pay for all our sins before the world began. He also lived the perfectly obedient life on earth. And His consistent, holy, obedient, perfectly-righteous life counts for you and me. Though we see ourselves in a daily walk that is often sadly lacking (and sometimes outright rotten and disobedient), the Father still sees us in the Son. "Even before He made the world, God loved us and chose us in Christ to be holy and without fault in His eyes" (Ephesians 1:4 NLT). When we come before the throne of God, we will come into His presence "innocent of sin and with great joy" (Jude 24 NLT).

These great truths apply to all who believe. "For if you confess with your mouth that Jesus is Lord and believe in your heart that God raised him from the dead, you will be saved. For it is by believing in your heart that you are made right with God, and it is by confessing with your mouth that you are saved" (Romans 10:9-10 NLT). "And you can't take credit for this; it is a gift from God" (Ephesians 2:8 NLT). In other words, God gives the gift of faith to those for whom Christ died, the sheep. If you believe, it is because He reconciled you to Himself before the world began. It is these profound realities of grace that empower us to live Christ-honoring lives in the here and now.

Oh Holy Spirit, do Your sanctifying work in each of us today. And we praise You that You will indeed conform us to Your image and present us faultless and blameless before Your throne of grace.

God is our Sanctifier

*And the very God of peace sanctify you wholly; and I pray God
your whole spirit and soul and body be preserved blameless
unto the coming of our Lord Jesus Christ.
Faithful is he that calleth you, who also will do it.
—1 Thessalonians 5:23-24*

Oh, what good news this is! God Himself is our Sanctifier, the
One who continually presents us as holy, set apart, counted as
blameless. Our sins are no longer counted against us if we are in
Christ. Day by day He keeps us blameless in His eyes.

It is interesting that the apostle Paul specifically spoke of
the body, soul, and spirit as separate strongholds for potential
sin. As long as we live in our physical body, we are faced with
the temptations of the flesh. John described these as "the lust
of the flesh and the lust of the eyes" (1 John 2:16). These sins
tend to be in the realm of the fleshly appetites—food, drink,
sexual impurities, etc.

The realm of the "soul sins" include sins of the mind, the
will, and the emotions. The Greek word for soul is *psyche* and

is often translated as *mind*. Jesus said that "whosoever looketh at a woman to lust after her" has already committed adultery (Matthew 5:28). The sins of our mind certainly include envy, pride, jealousy, adultery, and even murder.

Additionally, the "soul sins" include failing to choose to do the right thing (*will*power) and often willfully choosing to do the wrong thing! "I don't understand myself at all, for I really want to do what is right, but I don't do it. Instead, I do the very thing I hate" (Romans 7:15 NLT).

Our emotions also create sin problems. We experience anger, worry, frustration, and other negative feelings that are not God-honoring. Thus, our soul life involves the mind, the will, and the emotions. Even the human spirit in us, though renewed by the Holy Spirit, still is drawn toward the way of the world. His Spirit is always jealously wooing us into submission to His view of the world (James 4:4-7).

It is only the faithfulness of the Spirit of God in us that continues to save us from utter ruin. "Now the God of peace... make you perfect in every good work to do his will, working in you that which is well-pleasing in his sight, through Jesus Christ" (Hebrews 13:20-21). It is His work, not only in our redemption, but in our daily sanctification, that allows us to come before the throne of grace boldly.

"For it is God who works in you both to will and to do of His good pleasure" (Philippians 2:13). It is the Lord Himself Who has committed Himself to the work of conforming us to the image of the Son. Those whom He chose before the world began are predestined "to be conformed to the image of His Son" (Romans 8:29).

Oh, what a Savior! He has not only saved us from the condemnation of eternal death, but He has also guaranteed that we will not be ashamed of anything in our lives when we stand before Him! "Whosoever believeth on him shall not be ashamed" (Romans 9:33; Romans 10:11). It is He who is able to keep us from falling and Who will present us faultless before His throne, with joy (Jude 24).

Lord, the Sanctifier of the saints, we praise Your Holy name.

Living Stones

The stones used in the construction of the
Temple were prefinished at the quarry,
so the entire structure was built without the sound of hammer,
ax, or any other iron tool at the building site.
—1 Kings 6:7 NLT

This is a fascinating truth. When King Solomon ordered the building of the magnificent house of God, the temple in Israel, there was to be no sound of human effort as the stones were assembled. All of the chiseling was done before the temple was assembled. Each stone was designed for its perfect place in the architectural plan God gave to Solomon (1 Kings 6:1-37). And after each stone was fully prepared, it was brought to rest in its assigned place in the temple.

What message might the Holy Spirit be giving to us as New Testament believers in this Old Testament truth? Remember, "All scripture is inspired by God and is useful to teach us what is true..." (2 Timothy 3:16 NLT).

How might the experience of those "stones" be significant for us in our daily lives? The apostle Peter provided us with some marvelous truth about this. He wrote, "And now God is building you, as living stones, into His spiritual temple (1 Peter 2:5 NLT). The apostle Paul understood this reality. He explained that Christ is the head of His body, the church, and "under His direction, the whole body is fitted together perfectly" (Ephesians 4:16 NLT).

The Greek word for temple is *naos* and it means "a dwelling place, an inner sanctuary." In the Old Testament the glory of God dwelled physically in the temple of Israel. Today the glory of God dwells in His people through the indwelling Holy Spirit. Paul wrote, "Don't you realize that all of you together are the temple of God and that the Spirit of God lives in you?" (1 Corinthians 3:16 NLT).

The day is coming when all the saints will be gathered together to form the fully completed body of Christ (1 Thessalonians 4:14-18). The home of God (His dwelling place) is now among His people…"the Lord God Almighty and the Lamb are the temple…" (Revelation 21:3, 22 NLT). This becomes reality in the glorious day when we as living stones will be assembled together. "Yes, dear friends, we are already God's children, and we can't even imagine what we will be like when Christ returns. But we do know that when He comes we will be like Him…" (1 John 3:2 NLT).

Until that glorious day, we who are alive are still in the quarry! We are being chiseled, cut, and polished in order to be fit into the place which Christ has prepared for us. This is the "prefinishing" work of sanctification, which involves the chastening, cleansing work of the Spirit. "My child, don't ignore it when the Lord disciplines you, and don't be discouraged.... No discipline is enjoyable while it is happening—it is painful!... So take a new grip with your tired hands and stand firm on your shaky legs..." (Hebrews 12:5, 11-12 NLT).

As Charles Spurgeon said, "All this is Christ's own work! Each individual believer is being prepared and polished, and made ready for his place in the temple; but Christ's own hand performs the preparation work.... Our prayers and efforts cannot make us ready for heaven, apart from the hand of Jesus, who fashions our hearts aright. No, we must be made perfect here—all that Christ will do beforehand; and when He has done it we shall be...brought to the heavenly Jerusalem to abide as eternal pillars in the temple of our Lord."

Oh Lord, help us embrace Your polishing hand today.

Sifted as Wheat

Satan has desired you that he may sift you as wheat.
—Luke 22:31

You may recall the circumstances surrounding these words spoken by Jesus to Peter. Just before the Lord went to be crucified, Peter proclaimed his commitment and unwavering allegiance to the Lord (Mark 14:29). Yet the sovereign Lord, Who knows our end from our beginning, told Peter that this was not what would happen. And, of course, Peter eventually denied even knowing the Lord.

Let's pause there for a moment. Have you sometimes made promises or commitments to the Lord only to see yourself fail? Have you had a deep desire to be faithful or to be consistent in your walk with Christ, only to end up being inconsistent or even rebellious?

If you answered "yes" to those questions, you will identify with what happened to Peter. In his fleshly enthusiasm and his earthly sense of strength and willpower, Peter felt certain he would never be among those who would "scatter" when the Shepherd was smitten on the cross (Mark 14:27).

But the Lord says a strange thing in answer to Peter's bold commitment. He calls Peter by his earthly name. "Simon, Simon, behold Satan has desired you...." The Lord knows Peter's weaknesses. Peter doesn't know his own weaknesses. And the Lord is about to reveal to Peter how weak he is in his human efforts to be faithful. Jesus explains to Peter that Satan, the evil one, has asked permission to test him, to reveal Peter's true colors as a weak, unfaithful follower of the Lord. And the Lord Himself has consented to this! Even in light of what was coming, Jesus said to him, "But I have pleaded in prayer for you, Simon, that your faith should not fail. So when you have repented and turned to me again, strengthen and build up your brothers" (Luke 22:32 NLT).

Oh, what hope we have in the midst of our battles with our flesh! The Lord Himself has prayed for us and continues every moment to intercede on our behalf (Romans 8:34). He will sustain us because He alone is the Author of our faith (Hebrews 12:2). And after we have suffered in our flesh and learned of our own weakness and turned to the Lord afresh, He will use us to strengthen other believers who are struggling in their weaknesses. What grace God extends to us.

The Greek word for sift is *siniazo* and it actually means to shake. When farmers wanted to separate the good grain from the chaff, they shook the wheat in a sieve. The large kernels remained in the net or sieve, while the unusable chaff fell to the ground. This is a picture of what the Lord is doing in our lives every day. He uses our circumstances, our fleshly lusts, and, occasionally, even Satan himself, to shake us. His purpose is to preserve us, to keep us from "falling to the ground" amidst that which is unusable.

The apostle Paul experienced his own battles with his flesh. "No matter which way I turn, I can't make myself do right. I want to, but I can't" (Romans 7:18 NLT). And Peter must have told Paul about his agony in denying the Lord. In response to the agony of failure, Paul penned these words of encouragement to us:

> If you think you are standing strong, be careful, for you, too, may fall into the same sin. But remember that the temptations that come into your life are no different from what others experience. And God is faithful. He will keep the temptation from becoming so strong that you can't stand up against it. When you are tempted He will show you a way out so that you will not give in to it.
>
> —1 Corinthians 10:12-13 NLT

Paul went on to tell us that God the Father is the One Who comforts us in all our troubles so that we can comfort others. When others are troubled, we will be able to give them the same comfort God has given us (2 Corinthians 1:3-4).

You will recall that after Christ's resurrection, in the garden of Gethsemane, an angel spoke to Mary Magdalene and the other women who were present at the empty tomb. The angel's specific words were, "Go your way, tell His disciples and Peter that He has gone before you into Galilee…" (Mark 16:7).

Isn't the Lord gracious to us, one by one? He knows us by name and extends His ongoing love and forgiveness to us in the face of our greatest failures.

Oh Lord, what love. Help us to receive it.

In the Presence of His Glory with Exceeding Joy

Now unto him who is able to keep you from falling,
and to present you faultless before
the presence of his glory with exceeding joy.
—Jude 24

Sometimes it seems we do not believe the incredible, life-giving truths and promises of God's Word even though we read them and hear them. These truths out of the little book of Jude are some of the least understood by the saints of today.

Jude was praising the Lord, Who keeps us, watches over us, guards us, and protects us, even from our own sins and failures. He has set a hedge of protection around us, and Satan himself cannot touch us except the Lord allows it (Job 1:10, 12 and Luke 22:31-34). We will be brought safely and securely before His throne of glory. We will not fall away. (The Greek word for falling is *apostasia* which is apostasy, defection from the truth, forsaking the Lord.)

The reason we will never fall away is that "He who has begun this good work in us will continue to perform it until the day of Jesus Christ" (Philippians 1:6).

The means by which we are being kept, or safely hedged in, is the power of God. We are "kept by the power of God through faith unto salvation ready to be revealed in the last time" (1 Peter 1:5). The Greek word for power is *dunamis*, the root word for dynamite. God's might is keeping us. His strength—not ours—is keeping us.

It is good to remember that faith is a gift. We are kept through faith, and even our faith is supplied by Him. "The life which I now live in the flesh I live by the faith of the Son of God" (Galatians 2:20).

Notice that in Jude 24 it is the Lord Himself Who presents us to the heavenly Father. He, our Bridegroom and our Advocate, will personally escort us to the throne. We will have a personal audience with the Creator of the universe!

It is at this juncture that many sermons have been preached on the dangers of this day. Many claim that if we have not been a "faithful, responsible" Christian, we will be ashamed when we stand before the Father. But what does Jude 24 tell us? The Lord will present us faultless before the throne. The Greek word for faultless is *amomos* and it means without blame, unblemished. I wonder if we believe this could be true.

We are sometimes told that because of our failure to accomplish enough good works or to have lived a consistent, faithful life, we will be ashamed at the throne of grace; yet Paul told us, "There is therefore now no condemnation to them which are in Christ Jesus" (Romans 8:1). Again, in Romans 9:33 and again in 10:11, "Whosoever believeth on him shall not be ashamed."

Our salvation, from start to finish, is all of Him. We do not contribute, in ourselves, one iota to the redemption process nor to the sanctification process. We are saved from the wrath of God by the death of Christ on the cross. And we are saved from a life of performance and self-effort by His sinless life, which counts for us (Romans 5:10; 1 Corinthians 1:30).

If we are in Christ, by faith in His shed blood, we are counted as a "good tree" and a "good tree" cannot bear evil fruit (Matthew 7:18). Our flesh may fail, but we are viewed as in Christ, faultless and blameless. What a promise!

Lord, we celebrate the fact that You alone keep us, protect us, and guard us from the enemy. And we thank You for the promise that You have arranged for us to appear before the Father, faultless and blameless.

The Secret of Obedience

Resist the devil, and he will flee from you.
Draw nigh to God, and he will draw nigh to you.
—James 4:7-8

In addition to these exhortations from James, we could add hundreds of others from the Old and New Testaments. "Pray without ceasing" (1 Thessalonians 5:18); "Quench not the Spirit" (1 Thessalonians 5:19); "Abstain from all appearance of evil" (1 Thessalonians 5:22); "Humble yourselves in the sight of the Lord" (James 4:10).

You, no doubt, can think of many others. Don't be envious. Give your money cheerfully, don't gossip or backbite. Don't judge. Obey the laws of the land. Love your wives. Submit to your husband. Don't lose your temper. Be kind, gentle, patient, longsuffering.

Are you exhausted yet? Depressed? Feeling hopeless, condemned, sinful, a bit of a failure? If your answer is yes, then you are normal. As believers, even though we think we understand the grace of God, the exhortations from the Word often create extreme discomfort in us. Why is that?

St. Augustine wrote, "God has given us commands that we cannot perform in order that we might know what to ask of Him." In other words, the Lord has outlined the daily attitudes and practical actions that He has designed to bring us the greatest peace and joy while we are on this planet. Yet our flesh often rebels against these exhortations because our flesh is focused on the lusts of this world, the pride of life. As believers, our only response is to confess the weakness of our flesh and ask for the strength of His Spirit in us to lead us into the life of true joy and peace.

Besides rebellion, another response is equally dangerous. Many believers think that through "self-effort and discipline" they are capable of living the daily Christian life. And if they are successful in being outwardly obedient, humble, etc., they often become proud of their own performance and very judgmental of those who, in their eyes, are failing to live the life of a believer. This, of course, is just another form of sin.

The question may then arise, "Well, then, how do you know that your obedience is from the pride of the flesh or the work of the Spirit?" Here's how we know. There is no good thing in us (Romans 3:10-20). And Jesus said, "Without me, you can do nothing" (John 15:5). If any good thing unfolds in our lives, it is His work, not ours. His grace keeps us from falling. Every good gift (patience, love, longsuffering) comes down from the Father above (James 1:17). Therefore, whenever we are walking in the Spirit it is a result of His power and His grace. We cannot take credit for one ounce of obedience and right living. And the Lord has a reason for that. He does not want to share His glory. "He that glorieth, let him glory in the Lord" (1 Corinthians 1:30).

Another powerful, yet rarely understood truth about these exhortations to righteousness, is the transforming power in their very existence. The Scripture says that faith comes by hearing and hearing by the Word of God (Romans 10:17).

The true meaning of *hearing* is to hear in one's heart and to obey. The Word is anointed with power and when we are exposed to it, it actually transforms us. We experience the faith, the power, the ability to respond because of the hidden power in God's Word. This is the essence of responsibility. This empowerment is manna, the daily provision by which we are obedient and walk in the Spirit.

Lord, give us the grace to come to You and to Your Word, day by day. May Your Name be glorified.

For His Glory

That we should be to the praise of His glory,
who first trusted in Christ....
—Ephesians 1:12

This is an amazing truth, worthy of much pondering and meditation on our part. The apostle Paul clearly stated that we are "predestined, according to the purpose of Him who works all things after the counsel of His own will," to have one calling in this life: that we should bring praise to the glory of God (Ephesians 1:11-12).

What does this really mean, Lord? And how is this accomplished? The Greek word for glory is *doxa*, to bring honor or praise, to worship. In other words, if we are alive in Christ, the purpose for our daily existence is to be the kind of person who causes others to worship and praise Jesus Christ, the Lord God of creation.

That is a humbling assignment. And the danger, it seems, would be for us to dare to assume that we are capable of doing this! Rather, our response probably needs to be a beseeching petition, "Oh Lord, glorify Yourself in and through my life today, please." And then go about our responsibilities with a heart and mind focused on Him.

In 1 Corinthians 10:31 Paul wrote, "Whatsoever you do, do all to the glory of God." This is helpful in a practical way. We can examine our motive for doing what we do in a given situation. If our motive is primarily self-centered, our activity will probably not cause onlookers to marvel at the Person of Christ.

Herod Agrippa I (son of Herod the Great, who was on the throne when Jesus was born) provides a sobering example of one who was totally self-absorbed. "Herod, arrayed in royal apparel, sat upon his throne" and gave a speech. "And the people shouted, 'It is the voice of a god, and not of a man.' And immediately an angel of the Lord smote him because he gave not God the glory: and he was eaten of worms" and died (Acts 12:21-23).

The Lord is jealous over His glory. He will not share it. Rather, we are to remember that our very existence, the fact that we have the breath of life, is because of God's grace. Our health, our daily bread, the roof over our heads, the ability to serve Him, are all manifestations of the glory of God. He is the Creator of all beauty, the Source of all life, the Supplier of our faith.

If there is a secret to having our lives reflect His glory and bring praise to His name, it may well be found in 2 Corinthians 3:18, "We all, with open face, beholding...the glory of the Lord, are changed into the same image, from glory to glory, by the Spirit of the Lord."

In other words, when we focus on the Lord's incredible glory—His goodness, mercy, and kindness toward us—our own lives shine. We are a reflection of what we focus on, day by day.

Too often it seems there is an emphasis placed on "what would Jesus do." This results in our own mental gymnastics to figure out what we think Jesus would do in any given situation. Sometimes that is a dangerous approach to living the Christian life. Only the Holy Spirit knows what Jesus would do, and the Lord often did things in an unpredictable way. When He went into the temple of God and cast out the money changers and flipped over all their tables and chairs, some onlookers must have been shocked (Matthew 21:12).

So our desire to live to His glory is best fulfilled by focusing on Christ Himself, the Word of God, and a life of worship. He will, in turn, give us daily wisdom and grace to reflect His glory in ways that only He has in mind.

Lord, thank You for placing Your glory in our earthen vessels that others might see You and worship You as the Lord of all glory. "God would make known the riches of His glory…which is Christ in you…" (Colossians 1:27).

The Faithful One

And I saw heaven opened, and behold, a white horse;
and He that sat upon him was called "Faithful and True."
—Revelation 19:11

Do you sometimes lose heart because of your lack of faith? And as a result of that sense of our own "faithlessness," we often become discouraged or depressed. The root cause of this negative experience is our focus. When we look at ourselves and have expectations about our own faith and faithfulness, we are often disappointed in what we see.

The Lord has given us a completely different way to live during our sojourn here in alien territory. It is He Whose name is Faithful. He is the One Who is Faithful to us. That is His promise as our Shepherd. He knows we are sheep, dumb and vulnerable.

In Hebrews 12:2 we are told how to live. "Looking unto Jesus, the Author and the Finisher of our faith." We know faith is a gift (Ephesians 2:8-9). Who gave us this gift to believe in Christ as Savior? The Lord Himself (James 1:17). Who will bring our faith to fullness, perfection, and completion? The same One Who authored faith in us will finish this work of faith.

In Philippians 1:6 Paul promised, "Being confident of this very thing, that He who has begun a good work in you will perform it until the day of Jesus Christ." It is the Lord Himself Who is faithful to accomplish His will and His work in our lives. In I Thessalonians 5:24 Paul again told us, "Faithful is He that calleth you who also will do it."

So, is it possible that we are looking for faith in "all the wrong places"? We are called to "look unto Jesus." He is Faithful. We are called to place our faith, our expectations, our hope, in His faithfulness, never expecting any kind of positive performance from ourselves. We will never be disappointed in His faith! And we can trust Him to accomplish in us what we can never live up to in our own self-effort or attempt at goodness. "For it is God who works in you, both to will and to do of His good pleasure" (Philippians 2:13).

Perhaps we experience weak faith because our faith has been misplaced. True faith is simply to believe in His faithfulness in our lives, day after day. "For all men do not have faith. But the Lord is faithful, who shall establish you and keep you from the wicked one" (2 Thessalonians 3:2-3).

Lord, enlarge our faith that we might believe in Your faithfulness. May we dare to believe Your Word. Anoint our ears and hearts to hear Your Word as truth. "If we believe not, yet He abideth faithful..." (2 Timothy 2:13).

Sovereignty

*In Whom also we have an inheritance,
being predestined according to the purpose of Him
who works all things after the counsel of
His own will.*
—Ephesians 1:11

Faith in God's Timing

But when Herod was dead, behold, an angel of
the Lord appeared in a dream to Joseph in Egypt saying,
Arise, and take the young Child and His mother,
and go into the land of Israel.
—Matthew 2:19-20

Timing—God's timing—is wonderful to ponder! It is awe-inspiring to recognize that days and months and years are significant in the Lord's unending work in our lives.

King Solomon penned these familiar words: "To every thing there is a season, and a time to every purpose under the heaven" (Ecclesiastes 3:1). This wise man went on to say that God's purpose and timing determines our birth, our death, our work, our weeping, our laughing, and our loving; even war and peace (Ecclesiastes 3:2-10).

"When Herod was dead...." This was the event that triggered the holy family's return to Israel. The Bible doesn't tell us exactly how long they had been in Egypt, but while they were there, they did not know what would determine their release from the foreign land.

Political events in Israel determined exactly where in Israel this family was to settle. Another evil king, a son of Herod the Great, was reigning in Judea. Once again Joseph was warned by an angel in a dream. He was told not to settle in Judea but to go to Galilee, to a city called Nazareth.

This was the fourth time Joseph had received direction from the Lord through an angelic visitation in a dream. Joseph never knew between these visits what the entire plan of God was for his life. He only got clear direction at the exact, critical moment he needed direction. Never early. Never too late. This is the nature of the walk of faith, waiting upon Him for the direction we need. And it will come, in His timing.

In his dissertation on the Lord's timing, King Solomon wrote, "God has made everything beautiful in his time…no man can find out the work that God maketh from the beginning to the end" (Ecclesiastes 3:11). We will never understand how all of the events in our lives fit together until we look back from heaven and see the whole of history. Meanwhile, we have His Word by which to walk in the here and now.

Joseph was led to return to his hometown, Nazareth. There he began (or resumed) his business as a carpenter. Jesus learned the trade as well. As far as we know, the next ten to twelve years were relatively uneventful in this family's life. No more angelic visits are recorded. Life was, perhaps, predictable. Mary and Joseph had at least six children after the birth of Jesus, four boys and at least two girls (Matthew 13:58).

Is it possible that Mary began to doubt what God was doing? Is it possible that she questioned whether or not those early promises were truly going to be fulfilled?

There is no record of Joseph's presence during Christ's adult ministry, which causes most scholars to believe Joseph died, and Mary was left to raise at least seven children by herself. Is it possible she felt abandoned by the One Who had worked such miracles in her life in the past?

As human beings, we do not find that believing the Word of God or walking by faith comes naturally. Rather, it is a supernatural way of living. In the human realm, walking by faith does not make sense. Yet when the Lord takes up residence in us in the person of the Holy Spirit, we learn to listen for the still small voice that can only be heard by believers.

Oh Lord, open our hearts, minds, and ears to Your voice. May we rest in Your moment-by-moment direction in our lives.

The Lord is our Teacher

I am the Lord your God, who teaches you what is best for you,
who directs you in the way you should go.
—Isaiah 48:17 NIV

Notice what the Lord says He does for His own. In His mercy
and grace He teaches us what is best for us. Only He, the Source
of all wisdom, knows what is best for each of us. Yet how often
we tell Him what we think would be best! We even pray for
outcomes, solutions, and adventures that we have determined
would be perfect for us. Then we sometimes hit a brick wall and
are often injured in the crash.

Does this sound familiar in terms of your life experience? It
is in the crash and the pain of injury we often look up for help.
These are sometimes our most "teachable" moments. It is then
we finally say, "Okay, Lord, what do you want to teach me?"

Deep in our hearts, as believers, we want what He wants for
us. And He is the One Who "directs you in the way you should

go." Our sovereign Lord is directing our steps and protecting us even when we are asleep (Proverbs 6:22). He will accomplish His purpose in us. "He works all things after the counsel of His own will" (Ephesians 1:11).

Amazingly, the Lord has not gone away and left us behind to figure out what is best for us or what we should do. He has chosen to provide us, individually, with a Guide, a Teacher, Who will accomplish the King's purpose in us. This Counselor will "guide you into all truth.... He will tell you about the future.... He will reveal to you whatever He receives from me" (John 16:13-15 NLT). This Counselor is "my representative.... He will teach you everything..." (John 14:26 NLT).

The best news is that the Lord has ordained our steps, including the crashes! "We can make our plans, but the Lord determines our steps" (Proverbs 16:9 NLT). He alone knows the end from the beginning. We are His jewels, His treasure. He has created us for His glory and He will accomplish His plan. He is love and He loves us fully, completely, consistently. He is interceding in our behalf every second. And He has given us Himself in the Comforter Who comforts us when we think the crashes are fatal to our life in Him.

Oh Lord, we praise You because Your ways are perfect. Thank You for being our wise Teacher. We embrace Your love and the future You have designed for us, even when we cannot see what that will be. We, by faith, believe You when You tell us, "For I know the plans I have for you.... They are plans for good and not for disaster..." (Jeremiah 29:11 NLT).

Resting in the Father's Arrangements

I have no right to say who will sit on the thrones next to mine.
God has prepared those places for the ones He has chosen.
—Mark 10:40 NLT

The Lord is forever underscoring that He has an ordained plan behind every detail of all that unfolds in heaven, on earth, and under the earth. In this passage from the gospel of Mark, the disciples have been quibbling over who will receive the greatest position of authority in the future kingdom. James and John, the sons of Zebedee, asked to sit on either side of the Lord in His kingdom reign. The Lord's answer reveals many truths to us.

First, we recognize our own humanity in the request these brothers made. We sometimes think we might be able to qualify for some reward in the coming age. In fact, we are sometimes led to believe that if we do enough stuff right, we can earn a place of honor. Yet the Lord says those assignments have already been made. The Father has ordained the future assignments of individual saints, just as He ordains who will come to Christ or who was called to serve as one of the twelve disciples during His earthly sojourn.

We also learn that the saints will indeed reign with Christ in the coming age. He will establish His kingdom and we will serve as joint-heirs with Him.

In addition, we learn that in His humanity, while here on earth, the Son was not allowed to know all the Father was doing ultimately. There were some things the Son simply did not know because He had chosen to become fully man on earth. In discussing the events that will unfold in the end of this age, Jesus said, "No one knows the day or the hour when these things will happen, not even the angels in heaven or the Son Himself. Only the Father knows" (Matthew 24:36 NLT).

Another important truth is that the Son trusted the Father's ordained (predestined) plan completely. He knew the Father's character to be the embodiment of love and wisdom. He also knew that the Father is sovereign, Lord over all. God the Father determines every detail in the universe, from falling sparrows to the hairs on our heads.

The Son Himself knew the Father's plan was not to be altered. Even at Gethsemane, as He prayed to be saved from the cross, He ultimately bowed His head to the Father. "Nevertheless, not my will, but thine be done." Christ had already announced to the disciples several times that He would die and be resurrected in three days. He knew the Father's will would be done, yet, in His humanity, He was free to fully express His human needs. However, His place of ultimate peace was found in trusting the Father's sovereign plan.

Lord, give us the grace to rest in that which we do not understand and rely on the wisdom of the Father's arrangements!

The Mystery of Prayer

The mystery of prayer and how it works can be one of the most confusing aspects of our daily lives in Christ. First, we have the humanistic idea that "prayer changes things." In other words, we are often taught that if you pray long enough or hard enough or with enough faith or with enough people, God will change His plans in response to our human prayer efforts. This is simply not true.

However, there is a sense in which prayer does change things. Here is how and why prayer can be said to change things: Prayer is God's chosen means for releasing His power to accomplish His purposes.

True prayer begins in heaven. God the Father has a plan. He sends His Spirit into our hearts and minds and we feel "moved" to pray for a particular person or situation. For example, you may be moved to pray for your neighbors who live two doors down from you. Eventually they come to know Christ. Did your prayers make the difference? Yes and no. The Lord moved you to participate in the accomplishment of His purpose. What a privilege!

However, notice in this example that you were probably not moved to pray for every single family on your block. That is because He was calling that family in particular to Himself.

In the Ezekiel passage, the Lord says He will see to it that Israel prays for what the Lord has already prophesied He will do! He changes the hearts of even hard-hearted, stiff-necked people (like you and I and the Israelites) to get in tune with His plan. He did this by moving Israel to pray for His mercy.

For example, Jonah prayed to be delivered from the belly of the great fish so that he could proclaim salvation to the Ninevites. This was not Jonah's initial plan. But the Lord brought him into a place of agreement with God's plan. Thus, Jonah's prayers were the means for releasing him from his desperate circumstances.

In John 17:24 Jesus prayed, "Father, I will that they also whom Thou hast given Me be with Me where I am." The Lord was headed for heaven and was praying for believers to be with Him there. Yet there are times when we see a loved one in a life or death situation and we want to pray, "Dear God, I will that he gets well and stays here with me." These are the moments when we need to remember that true prayer is when we listen for His direction, His will, not ours.

An early twentieth century saint wrote, "If only prayer in accord with God's will is fulfilled, why pray at all?...The answer is simple: Prayer is an essential part of God's ordained program.... God is engaged in drawing His creatures to Himself by various means.... Prayer does not originate with us, but with Him.... Prediction (of what is ordained) does not dispense with prayer, it draws it out."

We know that the apostle John wrote the entire book of Revelation giving the prophetic details, the timing, and the events related to Christ's second coming. And what is John's closing statement? A prayer! "Even so, come, Lord Jesus" (Revelation 22:20). John prayed for what he knew would eventually happen.

The exciting reality is that when the Lord moves us to pray for someone or for some situation, we can be expectant about the results! He is initiating our concern or our interest or our sense of "burden." That is because He is involving us in accomplishing what He has already ordained. John Piper said, "The Lord asks us to do what only He can do!" In other words, He asks us to preach the gospel, to pray for healing or salvation or protection or whatever is on our hearts, but only He can accomplish the results!

The purpose of prayer is not for us to dictate to God what we want Him to do. He alone knows the end from the beginning. His purposes will be accomplished, and they will be perfect.

It is often our humanistic way of thinking that creates our frustration with what appears to be "unanswered" prayer. Or we think we should have prayed harder and longer and thereby changed the outcome of a situation. Yet we read that the God of Israel "is not human that He should change His mind" (1 Samuel 15:29 NLT).

As Charles Spurgeon wrote, "Be thou content to leave thy prayer in His hands, who knows when to give, and how to give and what to give and what to withhold."

Lord, teach us to listen more intently so that we might join You in Your plans, prayerfully.

Set Free... While Sleeping

I the Lord have called thee...to open the blind eyes,
to bring out the prisoners from the prison,
and them that sit in darkness out of the prison house.
—Isaiah 42:6-7

God the Father is speaking to His servant, God the Son, in this passage. We learn that Christ will come to set prisoners free and bring them out of the darkness of their prison house. And God is describing the condition of all humans outside of Christ. We are held captive by Satan, enslaved to him, chained in darkness until we are rescued by Christ Himself.

In Colossians 1:13 Paul said that the Father "has delivered us from the power of darkness and hath translated us into the kingdom of His dear Son." We have been set free by the Son's redemptive work on our behalf.

Acts 12:5-18 paints a marvelous picture of what has happened to us as believers. It is portrayed in the actual events Peter experienced. Peter was taken prisoner by Herod (who is a picture of Satan and the bondage of the law at work). He was chained to two soldiers and placed under the watch of sixteen guards. The prison was filled with darkness. Escape was humanly impossible. He was scheduled to go to trial the next morning and be condemned to death.

This situation, of course, depicts our condition outside of Christ. We are guilty of breaking God's laws. Satan has us bound because of that, and we are condemned to die. We are held captive, in spiritual darkness, with no hope of escape.

In Acts 12:6-7 we read that while Peter was asleep a miracle suddenly occurred. An angel of the Lord came to him; a light shone in the darkness. The angel of the Lord "raised him up, saying 'Arise up quickly' and his chains fell off…."

Isn't it amazing to see that Peter was asleep, having no knowledge that he was about to be rescued? He certainly did not contribute to the rescue! Peter was stunned by this miraculous deliverance. The angelic messenger told him to "Gird thyself, and bind on thy sandals…cast thy garment about thee and follow me."

As Peter followed the angel, every door was opened miraculously, including the huge iron gate that protected the entire city. At this point Peter finally realized what had happened. "The Lord has sent his angel and saved me…" (Acts 12:11 NLT).

The apostle Paul wrote to the Ephesians with the same angelic message. "Awake thou that sleepest, and arise from the dead, and Christ shall give thee light" (Ephesians 5:14). The Lord's call wakes us from our sleep. He shines the light of the gospel into our hearts and we are set free from sin and darkness. This is the gospel of the grace of God (Acts 20:24).

Paul also instructed delivered saints to gird ourselves with truth and be sure our feet are shod with the gospel of peace (Ephesians 6:14-15). We have been clothed in the garment of His righteousness and we are now free to follow Him. The gates of the heavenly city of Jerusalem are open to us!

Our personal deliverance from the penalty of death is a miracle. We have been set free, redeemed from an eternity separated from the Savior. And all of this was arranged while we were yet sleeping.

Lord, we fall on our faces when we think of this incredible act of Your sovereign grace on our behalf.

Saved and then Called

Who hath saved us, and called us with a holy calling.
—2 Timothy 1:9

The Spirit of God reveals the heart and truth of the Father in His Word. And often, He teaches us amazing truth through even the order or arrangement of the written Word. In this passage from Paul's second letter to Timothy, it is significant that the Lord saves us first. Then He calls those He has saved!

Paul taught this miraculous reality again and again. In Romans 8:30 we read, "Moreover whom He did predestinate, them He also called...." We were His by His choosing before we responded to His call. And He only calls those He has already saved!

In the book of Acts, Luke taught this same truth. In Acts 13:48 he wrote, "And as many as were ordained to eternal life believed." The Greek word for ordained is *tasso* which means appointed or selected.

In Matthew chapter 22, Jesus Himself gives a parable that reveals a significant truth about being called. He tells of a king who invites people to his son's marriage feast. The call, the invitation, goes out to many people. But they all have reasons why they decline the invitation. They are basically busy with their own lives.

Then the king sends his servants to gather another group of people and these accept the invitation. Jesus concludes this strange parable by saying, "Many are called, but few are chosen" (Matthew 22:14). The Greek word for chosen is *ekletos,* sometimes translated *elected.* The elect of God are those who are chosen by Him. God is the King in the parable. His Son is getting married. The invitation to the marriage feast continues to go out and is heard by many in the world today. Yet most apparently hear with the physical ear only.

In the parable of Matthew 13, Jesus teaches that the ears that hear spiritual truth are the ears of the elect, those who have been predestined to believe (Matthew 13:10-16, 43). Faith is a gift and comes to us through the "hearing of the Word" (Romans 10:17). The Lord alone opens our ears to hear.

The great nineteenth century preacher, Charles Haddon Spurgeon, commented on 2 Timothy 1:9 ("Who hath saved us, and called us with an holy calling"). He said that believers are "perfectly saved in God's purpose.... God neither chose them nor called them because they were holy, but He called them that they might be holy, and holiness is the beauty produced by His workmanship in them. The excellencies we see in a believer are as much the work of God as the atonement itself."

It is the magnificence (and the mystery) of the Lord's grace that brings us to His throne with joy and thanksgiving.

Oh Lord, open our eyes as well as our ears that we might see the wonders in Your Word.

Heart Surgery

The Lord opened her heart to give heed to what was said....
—Acts 16:14 RSV

The Word of God has a lot to say about the heart. The condition of the heart of every human is described in Jeremiah 17:9, "The heart is deceitful above all things, and desperately wicked." The Lord confirms this in the New Testament. "For out of the heart proceed evil thoughts, murders, adulterers, fornicators, thefts, false witness, blasphemies..." (Matthew 15:19). That sounds like the ultimate in wickedness, doesn't it?

In the book of Romans, Paul described "the lusts" of the heart, the "hardness and impenitent heart." He suggests that the heart needs to be circumcised, to undergo surgery (Romans 1:24, 2:5, 29).

Ezekiel, the prophet, described the heart of the natural man as "whorish," "stony," and idolatrous (Ezekiel 6:9, 11:19, 14:3-4).

King Solomon described the natural man as one who has a heart that "studies destruction" (Proverbs 24:2). The Lord described the religious people of His day and said, "These people honor me with their lips but their hearts are far from me" (Mark 7:6 NIV).

Isn't it remarkable that the Lord determines our condition based on what He sees in our hearts, the very center of who we are? The Greek word for heart is *kardia*. And we know, physically, when we have cardiac illness, our very lives are at risk. The Lord says our spiritual lives are at risk because of the spiritual heart disease present in every human being.

It is interesting that most people think they can "fix themselves up" spiritually. Some believe that doing good deeds, being kind, or being charitable will qualify them for spiritual health. But the Lord says outward activity will not cure a diseased heart. Or we are often told we just need to make better choices and be more responsive and obedient to the things of God. Yet a deceitful, desperately wicked heart is incapable of being authentically responsive to God.

So what is the answer? God Himself has to give us a new heart. He literally has to perform major heart surgery on us, individually. Not one of us can operate on ourselves. We cannot change our own hearts. Even a heart surgeon cannot perform physical surgery on his or her own heart. The same is true regarding our inability to perform spiritual heart surgery on ourselves. It is impossible.

The sovereign Lord of the universe must invade our hearts. And when He does He says, "A new heart also will I give you, and a new spirit will I put within you; I will take away the stony heart of your flesh...and I will cause you to walk in My statutes" (Ezekiel 36:26-27). Jeremiah writes of God's sovereign work also. The Lord God says, "I will give them a heart to know Me, that I am the Lord…they shall return unto me with their whole heart" (Jeremiah 24:7).

We see how this transplant works in the story of Lydia in Acts 16:12-15. The apostle Paul had recently arrived in the city of Philippi. On the Sabbath he journeyed outside the city to a place where the believers gathered for prayer by a river. Paul and his friends began to visit with a group of women who were there. One of the women, Lydia, was a successful entrepreneur, a seller of very valuable purple dye. She heard Paul talking about the truths of the Word of God. And we read, "whose heart the Lord opened" so that she paid close attention to what Paul was teaching. She believed the truths of Christ as Savior and asked to be baptized as a believer. Lydia heard the truth because God sovereignly opened up her heart to hear.

Paul called the message he preached "the word of faith." He quoted Moses who said, "The Word is near you, even in your mouth and in your heart" (Romans 10:8). Paul then described how we believe: "For with the heart man believes unto righteousness; and with the mouth confession is made unto salvation" (Romans 10:10). We are to "believe in our hearts." Only those who have had heart surgery have a heart able to hear and believe.

Jesus said, "Those things which proceed out of the mouth come forth from the heart" (Matthew 15:18). Therefore, Paul concluded that if we believe in our heart we will confess Christ with our mouth.

There is much for us to learn here, especially in the realm of prayer. When we have friends and loved ones who do not confess

Christ as their Lord, we need to pray that the Lord would open their hearts to receive His Word.

Lord, we praise You for giving us new hearts. We are so grateful for Your surgery!

Born of the Spirit

*Just as you can hear the wind but can't tell where it comes from
or where it is going, so you can't explain
how people are born of the Spirit.*
—John 3:8 NLT

In John chapter 3 we meet Nicodemus, a law-keeping, Bible-reading, religious leader in the Jewish community. He knew his Old Testament from memory. He was a Pharisee, a chief rabbi. Yet Jesus announced to Nicodemus, this religious, God-fearing man, that he would never even see the kingdom of God unless he was "born again" (John 3:3 NLT).

Nicodemus expressed his confusion about what Jesus was saying. Christ elaborated, "Humans can reproduce only human life, but the Holy Spirit gives new life from heaven" (John 3:6 NLT). The Lord revealed an incredible secret to Nicodemus. No natural human being can go to heaven. The Spirit of God has to create a new being, a new creation, that is heavenly in nature. The "old person" dies, and a new person, a heavenly person, is created (2 Corinthians 5:17; Galatians 2:20).

Again Nicodemus was puzzled. He wanted to know how this works. Would he have to return to his mother's womb in order to be born again? Jesus startled Nicodemus with His mystifying answer from John 3:8. He simply said it is impossible to explain how people are born of the Spirit and made a new creation!

The news the Lord gave Nicodemus is also shocking even to the Bible-believing Christian world of today. Jesus explained that the wind blows sovereignly and no human being can control it. The Holy Spirit blows on whom He will and the new birth results.

In our physical births as babies, we had no control whatsoever. God sovereignly created us and placed us in the wombs of our mothers. He decided where we would be born geographically, when we would be born into history, and even our physical and mental condition at birth. He alone determined who would be our parents. The exact same sovereign Lord determines who will be born of the Spirit.

The apostle John knew this truth and wrote, "But as many as received him, to them gave he power to become the sons of God, even to them that believe on his name; who were born, not of blood, nor of the will of the flesh, nor of the will of man, but of God" (John 1:12-13).

The apostle Paul described this new birth by saying, "No one is able to say, Jesus is Lord, except by the Holy Spirit" (1 Corinthians 12:3b NLT). Jesus' brother, the apostle James, describes how the Lord engineers this new life in us. "Of his own will he conceived us with the word of truth" (James 1:18). The word of truth is here depicted as the seed of spiritual sperm through which the new birth occurs, with the Father choosing to create this new life.

Heaven is populated with sinners who have been cleansed from all their sin by faith in the shed blood of Jesus Christ, Who paid for the sins of all who believe in Him. Those are the heavenly beings who are born again by the sovereign work of the Holy Spirit. This incredible privilege of becoming a citizen of heaven is a result of nothing we could do by human effort any more than we could have orchestrated our physical birth before we were born! The faith to believe is a gift from God (Ephesians 2:8-9). We cannot produce faith. Faith is given to us by the sovereign power of the Holy Spirit. We then have eyes to see Who Jesus is and we confess Him as Lord, the result of the gift of faith.

Lord, we praise You for the grace and mercy You have given us that we might be given the eyes to see Who You are and a new heart with which to believe.

Unaided Omnipotence

Our sufficiency is of God.
—2 Corinthians 3:5

Are there times in your life when you want to just "give up" on some dream, or hope, or project, or heart's desire? Maybe you have prayed for years about a situation or you have longed to serve the Lord in a particular way, or you have wished you had different circumstances or the "right" resources, gifts, or talents to accomplish some specific goal.

Discouragement is one of the great tools of the enemy in our lives. And one of the reasons Satan is very successful in this area of attack is because we have a flawed belief system. In spite of what we may know theologically, a part of our flesh-bound humanity thinks we ought to be able to change things or accomplish something or achieve some goal. We may pray over whatever is the issue, but then we begin to try to "make it happen," whatever the "it" may be. Perhaps it is seeing a loved one come to Christ. You find yourself scheming on how to make that happen. Or you may want to improve your marriage relationship. So you read books on the subject and try to make a meaningful difference.

In all of these scenarios we sometimes see amazing, miraculous events unfold and we are encouraged in our walk with the Lord. But when nothing seems to change and all our efforts seem hopeless, it is then that the enemy attacks. One of the lies Satan tells us is that "if only you had…or hadn't…done this or that," then God would have answered your prayers. Or the accuser says, "If you were a more committed Christian…or if you were tithing…or if you hadn't made those terrible choices earlier in your life…." And we believe the lies he brings to mind because we still have some confidence in our own ability to contribute to the work of God. We do not really believe that all that is of value in His eyes is what He alone accomplishes.

Charles Spurgeon, in preaching on this topic, gave the example of Moses in the wilderness leading six hundred thousand Israelite men and their families, who are clamoring for meat. The Lord tells Moses, "I will give them a month's supply of meat." Now Moses simply can't believe such a thing is possible. He responds, "All the fish in the sea aren't enough to feed these people. All the animals in all our herds and flocks aren't enough, God!" And the Lord answered, "Is the Lord's hand waxed short? Thou shalt see now whether My Word shall come to pass unto thee or not" (Numbers 11:21-23).

Spurgeon then added his encouraging commentary. "Moses, overtaken by a fit of unbelief, looks to the outward means of solving this problem…. But does the Creator expect the creature to fulfill His promise? No. He who makes the promise fulfills it by His own UNAIDED OMNIPOTENCE. His promises do not depend upon the cooperation of the puny strength of man!"

Oh, what a flood of heartfelt faith and relief comes pouring into our lives when we really see this. It is God's UNAIDED OMNIPOTENCE that is the sole source of all that unfolds in our lives. He alone works all things together to accomplish His own will. Oh, yes, He works through human beings, but He doesn't depend on us or expect us to do "our part." He simply omnipotently and sovereignly orchestrates all the people and all the possibilities into one grand symphony for His own glory. He alone is sufficient. He is our sufficiency! God Himself is enough; we only need to know Him. If we truly know Him as the all-sufficient One, we are able to rest in Him, knowing that He will arrange every detail of our lives in harmony with His will.

The apostle Paul wrote about why God works in this way. "God has chosen the foolish things of the world to confound the wise... that no flesh should glory in His presence.... He that glories, let him glory in the Lord" (1 Corinthians 1:27-31). And in Romans 16:27 LB, "To God, who alone is wise, be the glory forever...."

Father, enlarge our hearts and minds to believe that You alone know the end from the beginning. And thus we can trust Your love and sovereign grace.

Freed from Sin

For he that is dead is freed from sin.
—Romans 6:7

The book of Romans is life-changing when the Holy Spirit unlocks for us the miraculous secrets buried in this magnificent treatise. However, without the wisdom of the Spirit it is easy to totally miss the amazing truths hidden here. The apostle Paul explained, among other incredible truths, the secret of freedom.

Most of us are familiar with Christ's words about freedom recorded by the apostle John. The Lord said, "You shall know the truth and the truth shall make you free" (John 8:32). The Jewish religious leaders could not comprehend what Jesus was saying (John 8:33). The Lord explained to them that they were slaves to sin, held captive by sin that would lead them ultimately to God's judgment and eternal destruction (John 8:35-44). Then

He repeated Himself, "If the Son sets you free you will be free indeed" (John 8:32 NLT). Jesus was explaining that a person is either a slave to sin (captured by Satan himself) or that person has been set free from sin and from the wrath of God that falls on sin.

Notice that the Lord told these religious leaders what the key to being set free is. "You will know the truth and the truth will set you free." Jesus said in John 14:6, "I am...the truth." The truth is a Person, God Himself. And He alone has the power to free us from sin's power and consequences. The Greek word Jesus uses for know is *ginosko* which means "to know by experience, to become acquainted with." These religious leaders did not "ginosko" Jesus Christ. They saw Him as just another rabbi, a teacher. And they didn't like what He taught. God, in human form, was talking to them; the Truth was speaking and they were arguing with Him.

Paul explained this truth about freedom from sin in Romans 6. "We died and were buried with Christ...and just as Christ was raised from the dead...we will also be raised as He was. Our old sinful selves were crucified with Christ...We are no longer slaves to sin. So you should consider yourselves dead to sin...Sin is no longer your master...Instead, you are free by God's grace" (Romans 6:4-14 NLT).

The question that must be asked is, "How did this death of mine happen? When did I get raised from the dead?" Herein lies the mystery of salvation. For you and for me to be set free from sin requires that there is a new, sin-free me that must come into existence. The old me, the sinner, has to die. Then the Spirit of God has to miraculously create a totally new me. This person is created sinless! As John writes in 1 John 3:9, "Whosoever is born of God does not commit sin."

Whoa! This is an entirely new truth that in our natural mind we cannot grasp. Let's review how the Scripture explains who we really are if we know Jesus Christ as God in the flesh, Who died for our sins.

First, Christ explained to Nicodemus that a miraculous work of the Holy Spirit is required for a person to be free from sin. "You must be born again," He said. By the sovereign work of God's spirit He actually slays the old you and creates a new you (John 3:3-5). He explained how this miracle happens. "The Son of Man must be lifted up on a pole, so that everyone who believes in me will have eternal life" (John 3:14-15 NLT). I become a new, sin-free creation of God by believing that Christ died in my place, on the "pole," for my sin. He rose from the dead, having conquered the captor, Satan, who had held me as a slave. Christ infused His life, His sin-free blood, into me. And I know it is true because I believe! Even my "believing" is proof that I've been set free because we cannot believe and call Jesus Lord unless the Spirit has already done this work in us (1 Corinthians 12:3).

The apostle Paul taught this amazing truth in his other letters also. In Galatians we read, "I have been crucified with Christ. I myself no longer live, but Christ lives in me. So I live my life in this earthly body by trusting in the Son of God" (Galatians 2:19-20 NLT).

Again, Paul explained that God the Father made Christ, Who knew no sin, "to be sin so that we might be made the righteousness of God in Him" (2 Corinthians 5:21). "Now you are free from sin, your old master, and you have become slaves to your new master, righteousness" (Romans 6:18 NLT). "So now there is no condemnation for those who belong to

Christ Jesus. For the power of the life-giving Spirit has freed you through Christ Jesus from the power of sin that leads to death" (Romans 8:1-2 NLT).

Have we really comprehended this truth? Have we dared to believe that we have been freed forever from sin? Do we believe that in the Lord's eyes we are counted as totally righteous, perfect, sinless? Never again will we be condemned because of our sin. This is the reality for those who confess Jesus to be God in the flesh. What might happen if we dared to believe God's Word on this matter?

Open our eyes, Lord. We long to grasp such grace.

A New Creation

*What this means is that those who become
Christians become new persons.
They are not the same anymore, for the old life is gone.
A new life has begun! All this newness of life is from God,
who brought us back to Himself through what Christ did.
—2 Corinthians 5:17-18 NLT*

It is thrilling to actually grasp that the Lord Himself is life. He is Creator. Nothing lives unless He gives life. Scientists today, for all their research and efforts, cannot figure out what life is. But the Scripture tells us. Life is a Person. His name is Jesus Christ. He said, "I am...the Life" (John 14:6). And we read in the gospel of John that the Word of God Who became flesh, Jesus Christ, is the Creator of all things. "He was with God, and He was God. He was in the beginning with God. He created everything there is. Nothing exists that He didn't make. Life itself was in Him..." (John 1:1-4 NLT).

In Genesis 1 the Lord brought forth life in the animal kingdom. Then Adam was created from the dust of the ground and God "breathed into his nostrils the breath of life" (Genesis 2:7). So we see the Lord as the Author and Creator of physical life. When Christ said, "I am...the Life," the Greek word is *zoa,* which means the opposite of death. It involves resurrected life and eternal life. This life is "the gift of God." "For the wages of sin is death, but the gift of God is eternal life through Jesus Christ our Lord" (Romans 6:23).

Why is this truth significant for us personally? The significance is multi-layered. First, listen to the words of John, "And this is the record, that God gave to us eternal life, and this life is in His Son. He that has the Son has the life; and he that does not have the Son of God does not have the life" (1 John 5:11, 12). We learn that eternal life is a gift from God. We cannot earn it. And this gift is Jesus Christ. If this life is not indwelling us, we are trapped in eternal death.

Herein also lies the secret of being "born again." The Lord creates a new life, a new creation, and places His Spirit and eternal life in those who believe that He is God in the flesh. (Even the believing is His work, for He is the Author and Finisher of faith and belief—Hebrews 12:2). The Greek word used here for new is *kainos,* which means "of a totally different kind or quality."

In other words, to be "born again" is not about reforming our attitudes or shaping up morally or becoming religious. It is about a totally new (different) creation being brought into existence. The prophet Ezekiel described this experience in the Lord's own words. "A new heart also will I give you, and a new spirit will I put within you; and I will take away the stony heart out of your flesh, and I will give you a heart of flesh" (Ezekiel 36:26-27). The work of salvation is God's sovereign work of grace in us.

And as if this creative, life-changing work of God were not enough, He went on to make additional promises. "And I will put my Spirit within you, and cause you to walk in my statutes.... I will also save you from all your uncleanness" (Ezekiel 36:27).

Ezekiel was describing what is going to happen to unbelieving Israelites when the Lord returns. And the process of this new creation is the same process by which He creates eternal life in every individual who is "born again."

Our very understanding of these truths is the basis for worshipping the Lord for Who He is, King of the universe. When we begin to grasp His sovereignty, we have a whole new appreciation for the term "amazing grace." In addition, we gain a new appreciation for the purpose of prayer. When we ask the Lord to reveal Himself to those we love who do not know Him, it is because He is the giver of this new life. He is the giver of life and He is the life. No amount of human logic or human persuasion can produce eternal life. We speak the truth of Christ to others, but the light is His to give.

Finally, when we begin to see that in Christ we are a different creation, a new creation, we experience fresh understanding of these words: we are "no more than foreigners and nomads here on earth" (Hebrews 11:13 NLT). We often feel as if we don't quite "fit in." That is because we are new creatures in Christ. What a miracle!

Father, we praise You as Creator, having made us into new creations!

All Things

*In whom also we have obtained an inheritance,
being predestinated according to the purpose of him
who worketh all things after the counsel of his own will.*
—Ephesians 1:11

There is something staggering in the truth that the Lord actually coordinates every detail in the universe to serve His own will. Nothing escapes His perfect control. The New Living Translation says, "All things happen just as He decided long ago." It is not only that He controls these details, He actually planned them. He ordains these details, having designed every detail before the world was created.

As if that is not mind-boggling enough, we read, "God causes everything to work together for the good of those who love God and are called according to His purpose for them" (Romans 8:28 NLT). The more familiar King James Version reads, "All things work together for good" for the believer.

Here we have one more miraculous truth. He not only controls all things and ordains all things, He actually controls and ordains for one specific purpose: He is bringing specific good into the lives of those who are in Christ. His entire focus is on His own family, those who are born again in Christ. He has designed the entire creation to bring His perfect plan for good into your life!

We read in Colossians 1:16-18, "For by Him (Christ) were all things created…all things were created by Him and for Him. And He is before all things and by Him all things consist…. He is the Head of the Body…the Firstborn from the dead…that in all things He might have the pre-eminence."

Here we see the reason the Lord is working all things together for good in our lives–we are members of His body and all things were created by Him and for Him. We are in Him and are therefore heirs of all His plans for His own glory.

And the Lord is actively involved in bringing this goodness to fruition in all things that have unfolded in our past, present, and future. In Ephesians 1:11 He is said to be working all things after the counsel of His own will. The Greek word for working is *energeo*, to be actively, efficiently involved.

In Romans 8:28 we read, "all things work together" for our good. The Greek word for work in this passage is *sunergeo*, which has the sense of helper or companion in labour. In other words, He is personally involved in working out the sometimes messy, and often confusing, details of our lives.

How might your life, or my life, be different if we were living in this reality every single moment of every single day? The great saints of old walked boldly in these staggering truths. King David wrote, "You saw me before I was born. Every day of my life was recorded in your book. Every moment was laid out before a single day had passed.... How precious are your thoughts about me, O God. And when I wake up in the morning You are still with me!" (Psalm 139:16-18 NLT).

Perhaps we need to find new words with which to praise Him for His constant *energeo* in all the things of our lives. "Marvelous are thy works; and that my soul knoweth right well!" (Psalm 139:14).

Lord, help me see that, truly, all that is at work in my life right now is flowing from Your sovereign, perfect, loving plan.

The Gift of Faith in the Midst of Darkness

Arise and take the young Child and His mother, and flee into Egypt, and be thou there until I bring thee word.
—Matthew 2:13

When King Herod discovered that the Old Testament prophesied the arrival of the King of Jews, he felt threatened. As a result of the visit of the wise men who followed a miraculous star, Herod did some inquiring from the Jewish priests and scribes. He learned that the birthplace of this King was in Bethlehem and had occurred several months earlier. Thus he sent out a decree, "Kill all the babies under two years old in Bethlehem and the surrounding area."

The Lord protected the Child by warning Joseph and Mary. He sent an angel to Joseph in a dream. The angel instructed Joseph to take Mary and the Child and flee at once to Egypt. "He arose and took the young Child and His mother by night, and departed into Egypt."

Suddenly, without any time for preparation or even any understanding as to why this trip was necessary, these lives were thrown into disarray. There is no record that the angel explained what was coming. The journey to Egypt was two hundred miles over desert territory, and their family and friends were left behind. The duration of their stay was completely uncertain. "Be there until I bring thee word," the angel said.

You and I may not receive direction from an angel in a dream, but we sometimes experience confusion and uncertainty when we find ourselves on an Egypt journey. We wonder why God has us in a particular situation. We wonder when we will be freed from uncertainty or discomfort. And we may even experience feeling abandoned by or disconnected from those we love. We have a sense of "being in the dark," even as Joseph fled "in the night."

The gift of faith was operating in Joseph. He simply believed the Word of God. He acted on the Word; he believed God knew what He was doing. He trusted the One he worshipped. And as a result, this family escaped the satanic plot that was unfolding by Herod's hand.

This same enemy, the wicked one, is plotting against us, day after day, hour by hour. Yet the Lord Himself has prayed that we be "kept from the wicked one" (John 17:15). When we experience darkness, confusion, and uncertainty, we have a way out—to dare to believe the Word He has provided. "Trust in the Lord with all your heart; and lean not on your own understanding. In all your ways acknowledge Him and He shall direct your paths" (Proverbs 3:5-6).

Amazingly, the Old Testament prophets had written that the Messiah would come from Bethlehem (Micah 5:2) and also that

He would come out of Egypt (Hosea 11:1). Only the sovereign Lord could orchestrate these events. This same sovereign Lord has written all our days in His book (Psalm 139:16). Our darkness does not hide us from Him, nor Him from us (Psalm 139:11-12).

Lord, give us faith to believe, to trust Your wisdom, and to follow You even when we don't know where You are leading, why the trip is necessary, or what the outcome will be.

Encouragement

And we know that God causes everything to work
together for the good of those who love God
and are called according to His purpose for them.
For God knew His people in advance, and He chose them
to become like His Son....
—*Romans 8:28-29a* NLT

Our Lives are in His Hands

Our lives are in his hands,
and he keeps our feet from stumbling.
—Psalm 66:19 NLT

Do you sometimes feel like you are "stumbling" along in life? With all we may know about the Lord's faithfulness, it seems we can easily be moved off the sure foundation of peace and trust in Him.

The apostle Paul said, "He is not far from any one of us. For in him we live and move and exist" (Acts 17:27-28 NLT). Every day, each moment, we are living in Christ. He is leading us; He is directing our footsteps; He is protecting us—even from ourselves and our own inadequacies.

"The Lord is my shepherd. I have everything I need.... He guides me along right paths, bringing honor to His Name" (Psalm 23:1, 3 NLT). Perhaps we need to set our eyes more often on the Shepherd and not so much on the path!

David, the psalmist, understood how important it was to count on the Lord's leadership and protection. In another psalm we read, "From the ends of the earth, I will cry to you for help, for my heart is overwhelmed.... You are my safe refuge, a fortress where my enemies cannot reach me" (Psalm 61:2-3 NLT).

Our daily "enemies" are often confusion, depression, self-doubt, irritation, and even a sense of being simply overwhelmed. These very emotions are joy-stealers from Satan himself. His goal is to fill us with emotions that move us off our faith foundation.

In fact, whenever our inner peace is disturbed we can be certain we are under Satan's influence. Paul tells us how to live each moment. "Always be full of joy in the Lord.... Don't worry about anything; instead, pray about everything...! If you do this, you will experience God's peace, which is far more wonderful than the human mind can understand. His peace will guard your hearts and minds as you live in Christ Jesus" (Philippians 4:4, 6-7 NLT).

Lord, help us! Our lives are in Your hands; we need help remembering these realities.

Stand Still and See the Salvation of the Lord

But Moses told the people, Don't be afraid.
Just stand where you are and watch the Lord rescue you....
The Lord himself will fight for you.
You won't have to lift a finger in your defense.
—Exodus 14:13-14 NLT

The Lord's ways are truly not in accord with our human approach to our challenges and problems.

In the situation described in Exodus, the Israelites whined and complained about their predicament. The Egyptians were chasing them, and wilderness life was miserable. The Lord's response to their desperation? "Fear ye not, stand still, and see the salvation of the Lord.... The Lord shall fight for you, and you shall hold your peace" (Exodus 14:13-14).

The Egyptians, with horses and chariots, were in hot pursuit of the Israelites. They were so close the Israelites could see them. The Israelites were on foot with no armor of any kind.

After telling them to stand still, the Lord's next words were, "Tell the people to get moving" (Exodus 14:15 NLT). Isn't this a classic picture of our daily dilemma in attempting to live the Christian life? We know we are to "rest in Him"; we are to "wait upon the Lord"; we are to "stand firm in the faith." But we have to get up and get moving every single day. We have to make critical decisions; we have to earn a living; we need to have wisdom for our children. So how do we both "stand still" and "get moving" at the same time?

The answer lies in the realm of the Spirit. Human wisdom cannot solve this puzzle. Something miraculous must occur for both of these actions (stand still/get moving) to take place at the same time. The Spirit of God comes into our hearts and minds with the gift of "blind faith."

In other words, in our hearts and minds we "stand still." We stop trying to "figure things out" or "get a plan" or "weigh all the pros and cons." Emotionally and mentally we just "stand still" and expect to "see the salvation of the Lord."

In the Exodus passage, the Lord told Moses what to do to facilitate getting the Israelites to move. (Remember, they were paralyzed with fear. The Egyptians were chasing them from behind and the Red Sea was in front of them.) The Lord's words to Moses in the midst of this impossible situation were, "Use your shepherd's staff—hold it out over the water and a path will open up before you through the sea. Then all the people of Israel will walk through on dry ground" (Exodus 14:16 NLT).

Don't you wonder what Moses thought about this "solution" to what seemed like an insurmountable set of problems? There was no human logic in the directive Moses received. Moses simply had to believe God knew what He was doing. Moses acted upon "blind faith" and the Red Sea parted.

There are theological arguments about the fact that true faith isn't "blind" because the believer knows and trusts the character of God. Fine. But we still experience being "in the dark" without any human understanding about what may be unfolding in our lives.

Our only response is to get up each day, make decisions, walk through our circumstances, and "stand still" mentally and emotionally, in the knowledge that the Shepherd's staff is opening the way for us.

Oh Holy Spirit, open the eyes of our hearts and minds. May we see that You are omnipotent, sovereign, and powerful over every circumstance in our lives.

Redeeming the Time

Redeeming the time...for the days are evil.
—Ephesians 5:16

Often when we read an exhortation in the Scripture we cringe inwardly. We are well aware of our failure to measure up to whatever we think the ideal Christian life should look like. However, Satan really has deceived us about the purpose of the exhortations, those calls from the Word that encourage us to change our behavior or focus our actions and thoughts in new directions.

The enemy has convinced us that every call to change our behavior is a requirement we must fulfill to receive more of God's blessings. And our flesh cringes at requirements. We don't like being told to change. Our response usually takes one of three possible paths. Either we rebel in our flesh and simply ignore the Word of God, we feel guiltier than usual and still do not change, or the disciplined among us may actually set some new goals and change behavior for a period of time.

But the truth is that behind each of the Lord's exhortations (His call to change or to act in a new way) is His Fatherly heart of love. He knows what will create for us the greatest joy, peace, safety, health, and happiness. For example, when He says, "Do not steal," He is encouraging us to avoid the pain and trauma of incarceration.

God is not saying, "I'll like you better if you don't steal." Absolutely not! He has paid for our sins. He has called us to be His own if we are alive in the knowledge of Christ. Like we do as earthly parents, He provides His children with practical direction for living what He knows is the most meaningful life.

Recognizing these facts, let's examine the exhortation to redeem our time. The Greek words enhance our insights into this passage. The Greek word for redeeming is *exagorazo,* which literally means "to acquire out of the forum." The *agora* was the marketplace, the forum, where daily supplies were purchased in the heyday of the Roman world. To redeem, then, is to buy up something of value.

Paul then told us what to buy. He wrote, "Redeeming the time…" in Ephesians 5:16. The Greek word for time used here is *kairos* and it means a fixed time or season. To use the marketplace metaphor, it is as if Paul were saying this is the season for avocados. It won't always be avocado season. There will be a time when they are no longer available. So now is the season to buy up avocados. In our verse, now is the season to "buy up" time.

Then Paul told us why there is an urgency in redeeming time. "For the days are evil." The term "the days" refers to a particular period of time. We read, "As it was in the days of

Noah," "There was, in the days of King Herod," etc. Paul told us that the times in which we are living "are evil." The Greek word for evil is *poneros*. It actually means "the evil one." Jesus taught the disciples to pray, "Lead us not into temptation, but deliver us from evil" (Matthew 6:13). He actually said, "Deliver us from the evil one."

Satan is the god of this world. Literally all that is unfolding around us is tainted by his deception and his war against the saints. The Lord, of course, reigns sovereign over all. Yet Paul reminded us, by the power of the Holy Spirit, that there is a reason to consider the reality of the times in which we live.

How do we redeem the "time" while we are in Satan's territory and we still have some time in our lives? Only the Lord Himself can answer that for each of us. Perhaps we can simply weigh how we "spend" the time God has given us. Are we investing or spending our time with activities that remind us of the Lord's love and grace and coming reign on earth? Or do we end up being depressed, worried, frustrated, or irritated over the news from Satan's realm? Perhaps we end up forgetting that the Father has a perfect plan and is working all things together for His good.

In Ephesians chapter six, Paul gave us some practical, Spirit-anointed wisdom on this topic. He summarized, saying, "Take unto you the whole armor of God that you may be able to withstand in the evil day" (Ephesians 6:13).

If we are being tossed about with fear, confusion, or doubt, perhaps our loving Father is encouraging us to invest our time in new ways during this season of our lives.

Speak to our hearts, oh Lord. Give us an awareness of how we are investing the days, the time You have given us.

Christ Alone is Our Strength

Without me, you can do nothing.
—John 15:5

The Lord spoke these words to His disciples as He was preparing to be crucified and ultimately ascend into heaven. Many scholars believe He shared these words at the Last Supper.

The Savior must have considered this to be crucial information for His disciples to know and live by as they survived in the world as believers. The Lord made this statement in the midst of His metaphor of the Vine and the branches. The branches certainly cannot exist if they are cut off from the vine itself, the root of the plant.

The Greek word for without is *choris* and it means, literally, apart from. James, the apostle, used this same word when he wrote, "Faith without works is dead" (James 2:26). By that James means that true faith results in good works, just as grapes are a result of the life in the vine feeding the branches and producing fruit. Grapes are the natural result of living grapevines. So anyone who claims to have faith in Christ but who bears no fruit is actually a dead branch, not connected to the true Vine.

The Lord encourages His followers to look to Him, the Vine, for their complete supply in all things. "Apart from me you can do nothing." The Greek word for do is *poieo,* which means to work in the sense of creating something. The Lord, for example, says we are His workmanship, His masterpiece or "poem," a result of His work, not ours. And all good work—all that is done by us as believers—will only have value if it is He Who accomplishes the work through us.

The Lord leaves no room for doubt on this subject. He says that apart from Him we can do nothing. Again, the Greek word for nothing is *oudeis.* Literally it reads, "You cannot do not even one good thing." There is a double negative in this statement. No, not one good thing!

So what does this mean for us on a daily basis? How are we to respond to the Lord, knowing that only He can ever accomplish anything of value in our lives?

Perhaps it means we should look up more often. We tend to look inward, trying to analyze what we should be doing, what we wish we were doing, what we ought to have done, what we have failed to do, and sometimes longing to figure out what to do that might be of value in the kingdom. Sound familiar?

Yet the Lord is giving us a platform, a foundation for peace. He says we have been cleansed, sanctified by His Word (John 15:3). Therefore, we are in Christ, we are abiding in the Vine because we are believers. The Greek word for abide is *meno,* which means to remain or continue. We continue, remain, abide in Him because He has promised to keep us safe in Him (Jude 24).

He then simply states that He will produce fruit in us. "He that abides in me, and I in him, the same bringeth forth much fruit" (John 15:5). Therefore, we can look to Him, by faith, knowing He is at work in us, accomplishing and producing all the works that have been ordained for us individually (Ephesians 2:10).

Lord, give us grace to believe Your promises. Lift our eyes from our own flesh, our own mental gymnastics, and fasten our hopes on You alone.

The Joy in Trusting

O Lord Almighty, happy are those who trust in you.
—Psalm 84:12 NLT

Isn't it amazing that Satan's primary activity in this world is to keep us from trusting the Lord's plan, the Lord's timing, the Lord's answer (or seeming lack of answer) to our prayers? Once again, the Hebrew word for trust is *batah,* which means to have confidence in the Lord's revealed Word to us, to confide in Him about our needs, wants, desires, and then to have confidence in His way.

The reformer Martin Luther wrote, "All my desires have not been gratified, but thy love denied them to me when fulfillment of my wishes would have proved my ruin or injury." The Lord alone knows the end from the beginning. His Word tells us that He loves us as He loves His Son if we are alive in Christ. His plans for us are "for good and not for disaster, to give us a future and a hope" (Jeremiah 29:11 NLT).

But we are often blinded by the ways of the world. For the world offers "the lust of the flesh, and the lust of the eyes, and the pride of life…but the world will pass away, and the lust thereof; but he that doeth the will of God abideth forever" (1 John 2:16-17). In this world of darkness, Satan's kingdom, we will never experience peace or satisfaction, especially when we get sidetracked from walking with a singleness of purpose in Christ.

Another Puritan writer, David Brainerd, described this reality. He wrote, "Thy never-failing providence orders every event, sweetens every fear, reveals evil's presence lurking in seeming good, brings real good out of seeming evil, makes unsatisfactory what I set my heart upon, to show me what a short-sighted creature I am, and to teach me to live by faith upon thy blessed self."

David, the psalmist, knew by experience that the only place of joy and gladness was in the Lord's presence, leaving behind the false pleasures and temptations of this world. "Happy are those who trust in you." The Lord Himself explained, "Your eye is a lamp for your body. A pure eye lets sunshine into your soul. But an evil eye shuts out the light and plunges you into darkness" (Luke 11:34 NLT).

Oh Lord, give us eyes for You alone. By Your Spirit give us a holy fear of Satan's beguiling lies that steal our peace, our joy, our gladness…and wound Your heart of love.

Open Doors and Closed Doors

Behold, I have set before thee an open door,
and no man can shut it.
—Revelation 3:8

Do you sometimes feel as if the doors in your life experience are shut? An open door often signifies hope, opportunity, direction, adventure, new horizons. Closed doors can produce the opposite emotions: hopelessness, lack of purpose or direction, even a sense of lostness or abandonment.

The Lord specializes in opening and closing doors. In fact, we are told, "He opens doors, and no one can shut them; he shuts doors, and no one can open them (Revelation 3:7 NLT).

Have you been pushing on some closed doors? Or have you been waiting on the Lord to open the right door? In God's grace He shuts some doors. He knows which door you or I should walk through. And He protects us by keeping some doors closed.

It is interesting to note that the ark designed to protect Noah's family from God's judgment had only one door. And this door was cut into the side of the ark. "And the Lord said unto Noah 'Come thou and all thy house into the ark'…and the Lord shut him in" (Genesis 7:1, 16). Noah received clear direction when the time was right. He was led through the open door. And then that same door was firmly shut to those who must have been pounding on it later.

In the gospel of John, Christ proclaims, "I am the door: by me if any man enter in, he shall be saved" (John 10:9). Christ is the ark of our protection; this door was opened by a cut in His side (John 19:34). As we enter into Him by faith in His Word, we have entered into an eternal relationship with the One Who is in charge of all doors.

We are the sheep; He is the Shepherd. He does the leading; we do the following. Sheep don't even know how to find doors. They would starve to death or be eaten by wild animals if left to themselves. The Shepherd knows the hopeless condition of abandoned sheep. He "calls his own sheep by name and he leads them…he walks ahead of them, and they follow him…where ever they go they will find green pastures…. I am the good shepherd; I know my own sheep (John 10:3-4, 9, 14 NLT). The sheep trust the Shepherd to lead them through the open doors to the green pastures.

Sometimes we even feel locked up, trapped behind closed doors. The Lord's disciples experienced this after Christ died. On Sunday evening they were huddling in the upper room. They were living in fear because of the religious Jews. The doors were shut. "Suddenly Jesus was standing there among them! 'Peace be with you' he said. As he spoke, he held out his hands for them to see, and he showed them his side" (John 20:19-20 NLT).

Closed doors are not a problem for the Lord. What is His message to those of us who are feeling trapped or fearful? Be at peace. I am here with you, even behind what may appear to be closed doors in your life.

And just in case the disciples missed this word of encouragement, the Lord repeated this lesson eight days later. Once again the disciples were together and "the doors were locked" (John 20:26 NLT). "Suddenly, as before, Jesus was standing among them. He said, 'Peace be with you.' Then he said to Thomas, 'Put your finger here and see my hands. Put your hand into the wound in my side. Don't be faithless any longer'" (John 20:26-27 NLT).

The One Who is the Door invites us to trust His wounds and the cut in His side as proof that we can be at peace. He will open and close the doors in our lives. He is the Shepherd Who laid down His life for His sheep. And He knows our names.

Thank You, Lord, for being in charge of all the doors in our lives!

Fullness of Joy

In thy presence is fullness of joy.
—Psalm 16:11

Have you ever pondered over the magnificent (but impossible to grasp) fact that Abraham ate lunch with the Lord face to face? (Read Genesis 18 again.) Can we comprehend that Adam walked and talked with the Lord in the garden of Eden? (Genesis 3:8-24). Or perhaps even more amazing is that some of the disciples sat with the Lord in His resurrected body and ate the breakfast Jesus had cooked for them (John 21:1-14).

Isn't there something in us that thinks it would be incredible to actually be in the Lord's very presence? The staggering, incomprehensible truth is: we are in His very presence if He lives in us by faith in His finished work. The Lord explained this reality to the disciples as He prepared to leave them without His visible presence. He said, "The Father will give you another

Comforter who will abide with you forever. And He will dwell with you and in you" (John 14:16-17).

The Greek word for another is *allos*, which means literally "one exactly like" the first one. If the Comforter was different from Christ Himself, the Greek word would be *heteros*, another, of a different kind. This tells us two things. One, the Holy Spirit is God Himself, just as Jesus Christ is God in the flesh. It is clear confirmation of God in His fullness, three in one. Two, this tells us that God Himself dwells in us and we dwell in His very presence. Right now. In this moment!

David knew that in His presence was "fullness of joy." Jesus told the disciples that His ascension and His coming to dwell in us by the Spirit was so that our "joy may be full" (John 16:24). Do we actually believe or remember that we are living in the actual presence of the one true God, the King of the universe?

Perhaps we can learn from David how to experience the Lord's actual presence. In Psalm 95:2a David wrote, "Let us come before His presence with thanksgiving." This is a wonderful means for accessing the reality of being in His presence. Just begin thanking Him for all He is to us. He is the Truth. He is the Supplier of all things—food, shelter, family, birds, flowers, trees, colors, music! Thank You, Lord, for all You are.

"Let us sing Him psalms of praise" (Psalm 95:2b NLT). The Lord's presence is also accessed through singing to Him. Paul wrote in Ephesians 5:18-19 (NLT), "Let the Holy Spirit fill and control you, then you will sing psalms and hymns and spiritual songs among yourselves, making music to the Lord...."

Lord, may we continually be aware that we are standing before You, in You, in this holy temple, in the body of believers. Then our joy will be full!

God Directs Our Steps

O Lord, I know that the way of man is not in himself:
it is not in man that walketh to direct his steps.
—Jeremiah 10:23

Somehow the saints of old seemed to grasp the sovereign power of God. They were very aware that God alone reigns over every detail of our lives. And He is orchestrating all those details together for His glory.

Those saints of old apparently had many of the same annoying and sometimes gut-wrenching distresses we have today. Job, in his horrific agony, cried out, "Let the day wherein I was born perish" (Job 3:3). "Why died I not from the womb?" (Job 3:11). "For my sighing cometh before I eat" (Job 3:24). Job definitely had some very bad days. He experienced hopelessness.

Yet the ultimate hope Job had was his solid belief in his future in Christ. He confessed, in the midst of his testing, "I know that my Redeemer liveth, and that He shall stand at the latter day upon the earth…in my flesh shall I see God" (Job 19:25-26). And he believed God was in all the details of his life. "Doth not He see my ways and count all my steps?" (Job 31:4). Job's solace was his awareness of God's sovereign reign over his life.

The wisest man who ever lived, King Solomon, had family problems, political problems, and personal agonies. He wrote, "A man's heart deviseth his way; but the Lord directeth his steps" (Proverbs 16:9). Solomon, in his wisdom, spoke again and again of our utter dependence upon the Lord's plans. "The Lord hath made all things for Himself: Yes, even the wicked for the day of evil" (Proverbs 16:4).

King David's greatest comfort and joy as in remembering the character of his Savior. "Thou art my hiding place; Thou shalt preserve me from trouble" (Psalm 32:7). For the Lord "forsaketh not His saints; they are preserved for ever" (Psalm 37:28). "The steps of a good man are ordered by the Lord…none of his steps shall slide" (Psalm 37:23, 31).

Surely we all struggle with our failures, sin, distress, frustrations, and the all-too-frequent condition of wondering where we are and what we are doing. The greatest (and only) comfort we have is to realize that God in His grace has ordained our steps.

Lord, it is not in us to direct our steps. We acknowledge Your wisdom and Your worthy plan for our lives. Help us walk by faith in Your faithfulness as You direct our paths (Proverbs 3:5-6).

Arise and Shine!

Arise, shine; for thy light is come,
and the glory of the Lord is risen upon thee...
darkness covers the earth...
lift up your eyes and see....
—Isaiah 60:1-4

The Lord has brought "the light of the knowledge of the glory of God in the face of Jesus Christ" to those of us who are born anew in Him (2 Corinthians 4:6).

As we continue to walk in Him we are transformed, day by day, by His light. "We all, with unveiled face, beholding as in a mirror the glory of the Lord, are being transformed into the same image from glory to glory, just as from the Lord, the Spirit" (2 Corinthians 3:18 NASB).

What did Paul mean when he said we have an "unveiled face?" He explained this as the removing of the blindness that prevents us from seeing the Lord's glory. He compared it to the veil Moses wore because his face so shone with the glory of God that the people of Israel could not bear to look upon him (2 Corinthians 3:7-9 NLT). However, this veil can now be removed through faith in Christ. Since we are believers, the light of the gospel has come to us, we have been granted repentance (2 Timothy 2:25), and the glory of Christ is shining out of us.

Paul also described us as "beholding in a mirror the glory of the Lord." The Greek word for beholding is *katoptrizo* and it actually means reflecting. In the New Living Translation it says, "And all of us have had that veil removed so that we can be mirrors that brightly reflect the glory of the Lord" (2 Corinthians 3:18 NLT).

What Paul said here has a fascinating, double-edged meaning. We have seen the light; this light is in us. So we are being changed "from glory to glory by the Spirit." The light shines brighter and brighter as the Spirit enlarges our understanding of "the glory of God in the face of Jesus Christ."

Paul also pointed out the way this change is being accomplished. As we reflect on the Person of Jesus Christ (behold Him), His image is seen in us!

Sometimes we attempt to "grow" in our Christian life by "techniques" we feel will help us be a better spouse, a more faithful student of the Word, a better pray-er, a more patient person. Often this only leads to an outward "shaping up" of our flesh, our self-life. Whenever we are "looking in the mirror" to see if we are shaping up, we are not looking at the glory of Christ.

True inner change occurs in our spirit as we simply look at the glory of God as revealed in Jesus Christ. As C. H. Spurgeon says, "We enjoy the blissful consequences which are ours because we are in Christ. These consequences which flow to us include His perfect obedience, finished atonement, resurrection, ascension, intercession as well as His dominion over all principalities and power."

God Himself "has blessed us with all spiritual blessings in Christ" (Ephesians 1:3). We are to rest in His Person, remembering that, "I no longer live, but Christ lives in me" (Galatians 2:20). We are called to behold His glory, His life in us, not our own self-life. "And the life I now live in the flesh I live by the faith of the Son of God" (Galatians 2:20). The Son is the Author and Finisher of our faith. And transformation—the increase of His brightness in us—occurs as we behold His life, His Person.

Father, let Your light shine in us and through us!

Never Separated
from Christ

Who shall separate us from the love of Christ?
Shall tribulation, or distress, or persecution,
or famine, or nakedness, or peril, or sword?
—Romans 8:35

This is a very critical question for most of us. When we are totally stressed over our circumstances or our unfulfilled needs (wants?), we feel pretty separated from the Lord's love, don't we? Yet these are the moments when we need to run into His arms, to hide under His wings of love and protection.

The apostle Paul listed seven situations or conditions that can cause us to feel separated from the Lord. First is tribulation. The Greek word is *thlibo* and it means to have troubles or afflictions that make you feel boxed in, trapped. Next he mentioned distress; the Greek word is *stenchoria* and it means to have anguish over your circumstances. Persecution, of course, is the experience of being pressed by others for whatever reason. Famine and nakedness are conditions in which many believers around the world find themselves. A peril is a danger of any kind—financial peril, danger to your physical well-being, domestic abuse, serving on the battlefield, fires, floods, hurricanes, shipwrecks, car accidents, etc. The sword represents life-threatening situations, especially related to battle.

Can you find yourself in a situation represented on that list? Paul was personally experiencing all seven of those challenges regularly. And it was Paul himself who, because of his own experience in Christ, answered the question he had raised. "Who (or what) shall separate us from the love of Christ?"

He wrote, "I am persuaded that neither death, nor life, nor angels, nor principalities, nor powers, nor things present, nor things to come, nor height, nor depth nor any other creature shall be able to separate us from the love of God which is in Christ Jesus our Lord" (Romans 8:38-39).

Paul actually added ten more items to the list of what might cause us to feel separated from God's love. He was convinced that not one of these seventeen situations can ever separate us from the love the Father has for His own. Nothing, absolutely nothing in our lives (not sin, not failure, not lack of prayer, etc.) can separate us from His love and mercy. Neither the angels nor the demons can keep us from being in the center of His love if we are alive in Christ.

Paul described God's love in such a dramatic way because he wanted us to live in the moment-by-moment awareness of the Father's never-ending love for us. "If God is for us, who can ever be against us?...Who dares accuse us whom God has chosen for His own?" (Romans 8:31, 33 NLT).

Perhaps our greatest challenge in living a triumphant, joy-filled life is that we ourselves are against ourselves! We condemn ourselves, accuse ourselves, and feel unworthy of God's love. We often walk in unbelief, failing to embrace these incredible truths from His Word.

May we dare to believe Him! May we run into His loving arms every moment of every day, in every circumstance.

Oh Lord, help our unbelief. Give us eyes to see You and give us freedom from our preoccupation with ourselves.

Only One Thing is Needful

Come unto Me, all ye that labour and are heavy laden,
and I will give you rest.
—Matthew 11:28

What an invitation! To think that there is someone who can dispense the gift of rest! The Lord tells us very clearly what steps to take to experience this reality of rest. "Come unto Me." There are many different Greek words for come. This one is *deute*, which actually is an insistent, one-word call. "Here!" or "Hither!"

The Jewish disciples had practiced law-keeping and good works all their lives as a means of trying to win God's approval. Christ is teaching them an entirely new way of living. And His message is desperately needed in our lives as Christians today. We are still under the false assumption that our striving to improve and our works of service will gain us points with God. Oh, we may not say we believe that, but we often live exhausting lives, focused on activity. We are busy earning a living, taking kids to school, serving in church, making time for friends, keeping up with daily chores, etc. Yet we often are not focused on the One in Whom we find rest.

The Lord is speaking about the labors of life here. "All ye that labour..." He is not talking about salvation. He is talking to those who already know Him. He is teaching them how to experience rest in the midst of a life filled with toil and "heavy" burdens. His invitation is to "all" who are seeking rest.

The Greek word for rest has its root in *anapa,* which actually means to "cease again." It is as if the disciples knew the source of the rest and needed to remember and return to the place of rest, which, for us, involves remembering we are in Christ.

Interestingly, one of the Hebrew words for rest is translated *Noah.* The Matthew passage in Hebrew would be, "Come unto Me and I will give you Noah!" Now Noah was a believer who lived and toiled and was burdened by the world around him. The Lord said to Noah, "Come, thou and all thy house into the ark" (Genesis 7:1). In the Scripture the ark is a picture of Christ Himself. The Lord actually invites Noah "in" to where He Himself is! God's call to Noah was "Come," which means the Lord was telling Noah He Himself would be in the ark. Noah and his family of believers rested in the ark, at peace, while all the world outside was suffering and dying. The picture reminds us that we are in Christ. He is accomplishing His purpose in us. We can rest in that fact.

In the Matthew passage Jesus goes on to say, "Take My yoke upon you, and learn of me." Each of the Jewish rabbis or teachers of Judaism had a specific focus in his individual teaching. And his disciples, those who were "yoked" or connected to a particular rabbi, practiced or valued that particular focus or emphasis. Jesus, as a Jewish rabbi, a teacher, is saying, "My yoke—my teaching—is easy. It produces rest. He does not say, "Learn this doctrine or do these good works or get your life together!" Rather, He says "Learn of Me."

You will recall the Mary and Martha story (Luke 10:38-42). Martha was busy serving (and resenting doing all the work!) and Mary "sat at Jesus' feet and heard His Word." Martha wasn't doing something "wrong," but the Lord saw her heart. Jesus said to her, "Martha, Martha, thou art careful (anxious) and troubled (agitated) about many things." Does that describe us when we are not "resting in Christ?"

The Lord is teaching about the condition of our hearts. Martha's heart condition, in her busyness, was one of being anxious, troubled, agitated. The Lord then says to her (and to us), "One thing is needful...." Wow! Don't we want to know what the "one thing" is? He tells us, "Mary has chosen the good part which shall not be taken away from her." On what had Mary chosen to focus? On learning of Christ. She sat at His feet and "heard His Word."

A little voice in us says, "Well, if I sat 'at the feet of Jesus' all the time, who is going to cook the meals and do what has to be done?" That is the "world's wisdom" speaking in us. When Christ was with the five thousand who needed to be fed and there was little food, He provided in the practical realm, miraculously. The greatest joy of the daily life in Christ comes as the Spirit teaches us that the Lord is enough. He is able to do "exceedingly abundantly above all that we ask or think..." (Ephesians 3:20).

So, even as we walk through our daily responsibilities, we rest in His abundant supply.

Lord, we hear Your words, "Come to Me." By Your spirit may we learn to rest in Your life, Your work, Your purpose, Your faithfulness.

Kept by our Father

I pray for them which thou hast given me....
Holy Father, keep through thine own name those whom
thou hast given me...that they also may be one in us...
and the glory which thou gavest me I have given them.
—John 17:9, 11, 21-22

The prayer of God the Son to God the Father in John 17 is simply thrilling. As we read Christ's words we realize that He, the Lord of creation, has made some incredible, miraculous requests to the Father on our behalf.

The Father and the Son are always in agreement because the Son knows the mind of the Father. Therefore, we can be assured that the Son's request on our behalf will be granted!

We will be kept by our holy Father. He will preserve us, never allowing the evil one to snatch us out of His hand (John 17:15; John 10:28-29). He will never allow anyone to speak evil against us at the day of judgment (Romans 8:31, 33).

It is His power that keeps us safe, day in and day out. "...who are kept by the power of God through faith unto salvation ready to be revealed in the last time" (1 Peter 1:5).

The Lord also has requested that His joy might be fulfilled in us (John 17:13). We may experience only bursts of intermittent joy in this life. Yet we will ultimately experience pure, uninterrupted joy forever. "In thy presence is fullness of joy; at thy right hand there are pleasures for evermore" (Psalm 16:11).

We will be sanctified by the Father because the Lord has requested this (John 17:17). This means that the Father Himself is certain to bring us to heaven, holy and blameless.

Perhaps the most exceptional request Christ has made is that we be one with the Father and the Son! We have been given the same glory that Jesus Christ has been given by the Father (John 17:22). And the Father loves us in the same way, to the same degree, with the same infinite abundance with which He loves His only begotten Son (John 17:23). In fact, John tells us that we are the sons of God right now and that when He appears again "we shall be like Him" (1 John 3:2). Certainly our finite minds cannot yet begin to comprehend the riches of these glorious truths.

Lord, grant us in Your grace the ability to comprehend what is the breadth, and length, and depth, and height of Your love for us.

Saved from the Wrath of God

Much more then, being now justified by His blood,
we shall be saved from wrath through Him.
—Romans 5:9

The apostle Paul never ceased being amazed at the incredible, miraculous blessings that are ours if we are in Christ. In his epistle to the Romans, Paul again and again described the specific elements of God's grace and mercy that are ours as believers.

In Romans chapter five Paul explained that "while we were yet sinners, Christ died for us" (Romans 5:8). And then, as if that weren't enough, he described the "much more." We have been justified by His blood, made righteous in God's eyes, and therefore, we are protected, saved from the wrath of God. This is another incredible aspect of what it means to have had Christ die for us while we were yet sinners! Paul wanted us to grasp the ramifications of this truth.

The Greek word translated as wrath is *orge*, the basis for our word orgy. This word is a description of the uncontrolled, incomprehensible, devastating anger of God. There is a time appointed by God when He is going to completely and totally unleash His anger on man's sin. Paul said Christ has "delivered us from the wrath to come" (1 Thessalonians 1:10). He said that "God has not appointed us to wrath" (1 Thessalonians 5:9).

The apostle John also described "the great day of His wrath" (Revelation 6:17); he spoke of "the fierceness and wrath of Almighty God" that is going to fall upon unbelievers (Revelation 19:15). The believer has escaped this horrific wrath of God scheduled to come at a time already appointed.

Paul continued in Romans and exclaimed, "Much more… we shall be saved by His life" (Romans 5:10). This is a truth that often escapes us as believers. We may understand that we have been saved from the penalty of sin through Christ's death. But Paul said "much more" we have been saved from the penalty of sin by Christ's life. What does that really mean? Why did Paul think that this is a "much more" truth?

Paul reminded us that Christ is alive, right now. He is eternally alive. He is sinless, perfect before the Father. And because we have been raised up from the deadness of sin, we have been made eternally alive in Christ. In the here and now, every single moment of our lives on earth, we are counted as perfect and sinless in His eyes. "I myself no longer live, but Christ lives in me. So I live my life in this earthly body by trusting in the Son of God…" (Galatians 2:20 NLT). This is the key to living the joyful, radiant life of a believer. We are counted as righteous every single day, even when sin and failure overtake us!

Paul continued to be thunderstruck by the greatness of these realities. Again in Romans 5:15 and Romans 5:17, he told us that though sin once reigned in us, "much more" the grace of God (and the gift of grace, Jesus Christ) has been shed on us abundantly. Because of the "much more" of grace, we will reign with Christ forever, clothed in His righteousness. And we have been saved from the wrath that is coming.

Oh Lord, by the power and revelation of Your Holy Spirit, open our eyes to see the manifold aspects of Your "much more" grace in our lives. And we give You praise for having delivered us from Your wrath.

Not of this World

They are not of the world, even as I am not of the world.
—John 17:16

The Lord makes this amazing statement about us as believers. He says that in exactly the same way He is not a citizen of earth, we are not citizens of this planet. I wonder what would change in our lives if we really understood this and believed it and walked accordingly?

The Greek word for world in this passage is *kosmos*. It refers to the arrangement of the world as it now stands. In 2 Corinthians 4:4 we learn that Satan is "the god of this world." In that passage the word translated world is *aion* which means age or eon. In other words, at this time in history, during this age, Satan rules over the cosmos. This is his realm. We are, as believers, aliens in a foreign environment.

The Lord declares again and again that the saints, those of us who know Christ, are from another realm. We are part of a heavenly cosmos, a completely different "arrangement," in perspective, in purpose, in truth, and in what satisfies us.

Satan is the father of lies (John 8:44). Therefore, the current world order is based entirely on deception. The god of this world continually teaches that in this world you can be happy if you attain enough money, marry the right person, achieve enough notoriety, gain enough power, or become attractive enough.

The apostle John gave us the Lord's perspective in 1 John 2:15-17 NLT. He wrote, "Stop loving this evil world and all that it offers you.... For the world offers only the lust for pleasure, the lust for everything we see, and pride in our possessions. These are not from the Father. They are from this evil world. And this world is fading away, along with everything it craves...."

The Lord's desire for each of us is to experience peace, joy, and purpose in Him. He wants us to enter into the "peace that passes understanding" (Philippians 4:7). As Christ prepared to leave this cosmos and return to His heavenly world, He said, "I am leaving you with a gift—peace of mind and heart. And the peace I give isn't like the peace the world gives" (John 14:27 NLT). He invites us to live in that peace by setting our minds on who we are in Him and intentionally protecting our minds and hearts from the deception and temptations abounding in the world.

When we experience anxiety, worry, depression, frustration, anger, and temptation, it is a result of viewing our current circumstances from the perspective of this world. We are measuring our life experience by the expectations of an "ideal" life that this world proclaims to be satisfying and ideal. Yet the

Lord Himself has told us, "Here on earth you will have many trials and sorrows. But take heart, because I have overcome the world" (John 16:33 NLT).

We can expect trials, tribulations, disappointments, and challenges because we are in enemy territory. But the war has been won. We can rest in the fact that the Lord is working His life in us in preparation for translating us, ultimately, into the heavenly cosmos. Meanwhile, our peace, while on this planet, is attainable only by viewing our lives with the mind of Christ, from His perspective. "Set your mind on things above" (Colossians 3:2). The word *set* in that passage means to have a fixation!

The Lord's brother, James, wrote, "Dear brothers and sisters, whenever trouble comes your way, let it be an opportunity for joy. For when your faith is tested, your endurance has a chance to grow. So let it grow, for when your endurance is fully developed, you will be strong in character and ready for anything" (James 1:2-4 NLT).

God, grant us eyes to see this world as the enemy's realm. Give us a mind set on Your realm alone.

The Mystery of the Universe

Oh, righteous Father, the world doesn't know you, but I do;
and these disciples know you sent me.
And I have revealed you to them and will keep on revealing you.
I will do this so that your love for me
may be in them and I in them.
—John 17:25-26 NLT

Being entrusted with a secret is important. And most of us are fascinated with mysteries. We have an innate desire to penetrate into hidden truth. The greatest mystery, the most incredible secret of the universe, has been revealed to those of us who know Christ.

In Matthew chapter 13 the disciples asked Jesus why He spoke in parables when He talked to the multitudes. Here was Christ's answer: "You have been permitted to understand the secrets of the Kingdom of Heaven, but others have not" (Matthew 13:11 NLT).

The apostle Paul was astounded to discover that the mystery of the universe had been revealed to him and to all believers. He wrote, "God's secret plan has now been revealed to us; it is a plan centered on Christ, designed long ago according to his good pleasure. And this is his plan: At the right time he will bring everything together under the authority of Christ—everything in heaven and on earth" (Ephesians 1:9-10 NLT).

The secret of the universe lies in the fact that God has revealed Himself in a Person. No one has ever seen God the Father. The secret is that God the Father has revealed Himself. He can be seen and known in His Son. "No one has ever seen God. But his only Son, who is himself God has told us about him" (John 1:18 NLT).

Jesus carefully and repeatedly revealed who He was to His disciples. He said to doubting Thomas, "If you had known who I am, then you would have known who my Father is. From now on you know him and have seen him!" (John 14:7 NLT). Then Philip said, "Lord, show us the Father and we will be satisfied. Jesus replied, "Phillip, don't you even yet know.... Anyone who has seen me has seen the Father" (John 14:8-9 NLT).

What is the practical significance for us, as believers, to know this incredible revelation—that Jesus Christ is God? It means that we alone have access to the throne of God's grace; we alone are free from the wrath of God which is coming on the world; we alone can stand on the promises of the Word of God; we alone can know that all things work together for good in our lives.

God the Father refuses to even hear the prayers of those who are not His children by faith in Christ's shed blood (John 9:31), those are the children of darkness, children of the world (1 Thessalonians 5:5). But we are not of this world. We are not earth dwellers. We are recipients of the knowledge that comes only by revelation, given by the Holy Spirit.

Lord, reveal anew to us the miraculous privilege we have of knowing You. May we treasure the revelation and abide in Your promises to us day by day.

Stand Fast!

Stand fast therefore in the liberty wherewith
Christ hath made us free....
—Galatians 5:1

The entire concept of freedom, of liberty, was foreign to many in the first century. In the Jewish religion, people constantly suffered under the bondage of attempting to keep the ten commandments plus hundreds of other civil laws. Failure to keep those had dire consequences, including stoning to death, thirty-nine lashes, etc. And in the pagan Roman world, slavery abounded. Only the wealthy Roman citizens had any appreciation for freedom. And the general population was under the rule of Rome.

The apostle Paul recognized that he was teaching earth-shaking truth to the Christians, many of whom had lived under the Jewish law their entire lives. Others were slaves who could not really even grasp the concept of freedom.

Paul wrote to the Galatian Christians in an attempt to educate them, again, on what it means to have been set free by Jesus Christ, never again to have to try to earn God's favor through keeping the Jewish law.

The Greek word for liberty is *eleutheria*. It is the very same word translated as free, *eleutherio*. In the New Living Translation we read, "So Christ has really set us free. Now make sure that you stay free, and don't get tied up again in slavery to the law" (Galatians 5:1 NLT).

Do you find yourself asking, "How does one stay free?" Freedom is an elusive concept. Somehow it seems we only know we are not living freely in Christ when we find ourselves living "under the law." What are the signs, the clues, that we have returned to the bondage of living by the law? They include self-condemnation, a focus on self-effort, striving to break bad habits or do good things, judging others for their sins, and measuring our standing with God by how well we have performed our Christian duty, which often spills over into our prayer life, church attendance, tithing, Bible study, etc. In contrast, the signs or clues that we are living in liberty include a joyful spirit, a desire to praise the Lord at every turn, an awareness of His presence, an overflowing love for others, a longing to know Him even better, and a bubbling desire to tell others about this life in Christ.

Where are you? Where am I? It seems we are constantly pulled into "performance Christianity." Or we are pulled into succumbing to the bondage of sin, which includes all the things the law forbids: anger, jealousy, adultery, gossip, fornication, murder, and backbiting. Notice that those sins are all of equal weight, i.e., they are sins. Sin is any activity not springing from the Holy Spirit at work in us.

The apostle Paul told us there is another place in which we can live. We do not have to live in the pull of our proud, fleshly striving to be good. Nor do we have to suffer in the misery of our sinful, fleshly acts. Remember, we are, in our new creation, free from sin. It is the flesh in which we still dwell that acts up! Paul had this very struggle himself. That is why he could give us the solution. He described his own struggle in Romans 7. "I know I am rotten through and through so far as my old sinful nature is concerned…. When I want to do good, I don't. And when I try not to do wrong, I do it anyway. But if I am doing what I don't want to do, I am not really the one doing it; the sin within me is doing it…. Who will free me? The answer is in Jesus Christ our Lord" (Romans 7:18-25 NLT).

What was Paul saying to us? What did he mean, "the answer is in Jesus Christ?" He gave us more clarity as he explained to the Galatians about how to stand in freedom, in liberty.

Paul said if you are in Christ it doesn't matter if you have been circumcised or not circumcised, having kept the law or been pagan. What matters is faith, your faith in the work of Christ, your righteousness which is a result of your faith in Him, in His life. If you are in Christ you are in His life, by the power and work of the Holy Spirit, so consciously live in that realm, the realm of the Spirit, by believing, having faith that "the life you now live you live by the faith of the Son of God" (Galatians 2:20). His faithfulness counts for you. Look to Him. Do not "frustrate the grace of God" by trying to shape up or please God by your own self-effort. Simply believe that your life is in His hands; the Spirit is at work in you. "For it is God who works in you both to will and to do of His good pleasure" (Philippians 2:13). "The just shall live by faith" (Galatians 3:11).

Faith is a gift from Christ, Who is the Author and Finisher of our faith (Romans 14:23; Hebrews 12:2).

We stand fast in freedom by simply believing the fact that Jesus Christ has done it all. His life lives in us—He, by His Spirit, is accomplishing His promises in us. This is the meaning and the means of being set free.

Lord, we praise and thank You for setting us free.

Affliction for a Season

There is wonderful joy ahead,
even though it is necessary for you
to endure many trials for a while.
—*1 Peter 1:6* NLT

It is interesting to realize that metal—steel, for example—is continuously tested until it is strong enough to serve in the role for which it was designed. Metal is not tested for the purpose of breaking it. It is tested and refined to make it strong so it won't break under pressure.

The parallel can be drawn in our experience as saints here on earth. The Lord, the great Refiner, is testing our mettle, strengthening us for the future for which He has designed us. So Peter encourages us to "endure" for a season because the end result is going to be awesome!

In the King James Version this verse reads, "Wherein ye greatly rejoice, though now for a season, if need be, ye are in heaviness through manifold temptations." It is fascinating to consider the phrase "for a season." The Lord has a time schedule, day by day, season by season, for accomplishing His perfect will for our lives.

We are familiar with the words of the wisest man who ever lived, Solomon, King of Israel, son of David and Bathsheba. He told us there is "a time to be born, and a time to die; a time to weep, and a time to laugh; a time to get, and a time to lose" (Ecclesiastics 3:1-8). What season are you in? God's Word promises that seasons in our lives will change. He has a rhythm in mind for each of us. The pressure comes and the pressure goes and we become warriors of the faith through the process.

Paul wrote to Timothy and encouraged him to "be instant in season and out of season." In other words, he told Timothy to stand solid both when the times are good and when the times are not so conducive to faith.

Paul knew what it was to experience severe trials and testings, yet he wrote, "For our light affliction, which is but for a moment, worketh for us a far more exceeding and eternal weight of glory" (2 Corinthians 4:17). Paul saw the reason behind the trials of this world. They produce in us "immeasurable great glory that will last forever" (2 Corinthians 4:17 NLT).

Paul also explained how to cope with our trials and testings by seeing our circumstances with the mind of Christ, from His perspective. Paul wrote, "We look not at the things which are seen, but at the things which are not seen; for the things which are seen are temporal; but the things which are not seen are eternal" (2 Corinthians 4:18).

The Greek word for temporal is *proskairos* and it means "for a season." Our key for living day by day in His peace is to look at what is unseen, not at our circumstances. And in His time, all will be well. "To every thing there is a season, and a time to every purpose under heaven" (Ecclesiastics 3:1).

Father, we long to see past our current trials and struggles and pain. Give us grace to endure and the eyes to see Your hand in all.

The Path of Life

Thou wilt show me the path of life.
—Psalm 16:11

How many times do we find ourselves longing to know what path we should take? Sometimes we long for the Lord to write the answer on the wall. "Here is where you are to go" or "This is what I want you to do." Yet the Christian life is about walking by faith, not by sight. We have the Light of the world leading us; and He knows the path we are to be on, day by day.

In 1637 William Austin, a Puritan saint, provided some amazing insights into what the psalmist is telling us. Austin observed, "There are four things to be noticed here: A Guide; A Traveler; A Way; A Life." The Guide is the Lord Himself. There is only one Guide to Whom we are to look for our direction. The Guide will show me, the singular traveler, the way. And this way leads to life.

It is interesting that the Scripture regularly describes us as travelers, as "strangers in a foreign land" (Hebrews 11:13; 1 Peter 2:11). It is easy to become lost when we are in foreign territory. We need a guide who knows the terrain and what lies ahead.

David, the psalmist, was very confident in his Guide. "Thou wilt show me...." David's life was filled with challenges and perplexities. On one hand the Lord had called him to be king of Israel. Yet King Saul was hunting David down to kill him. He was often living in dark caves in the wilderness. Nevertheless, he confidently said, "Thou wilt show me...." Lord, give us such expectant faith!

Notice that Jehovah will show us the path. This is not a freeway, or a highway, or even a road. It is a footpath; a narrow path that requires walking, one step at a time. The Lord seemed to be saying something similar to His disciples. "Narrow is the way which leads unto life, and few there be that find it" (Matthew 7:14). This path has a destination. The destination is life and only those who have the Guide will reach the destination.

It is significant that the traveler seems to be traveling alone with only the Guide's presence. There is a sense of loneliness, a kind of solitude. No others seem to be present to cheer or to give advice or direction or encouragement. When we experience our greatest faith challenges, we often feel quite alone. This is when we most need to lean on the Guide for conversation and confidence.

The other path is wide and broad with many travelers on it. Lots of company. Lots of advice. Lots of entertainment. That is the path that "leads to destruction" (Matthew 7:13). No wonder we sometimes feel as if we are "missing all the fun" or "missing all the money" or "missing out on life's pleasures." The crowd is some place we aren't!

The path we are on, if we are in Christ, is the path, the way, that is true life. We are walking in the way. This was what the Lord was revealing when He said, "I am the way, the truth and the life" (John 14:6). He is both the Path and the Life. We are both in Him and with Him on the walk if we know Jesus Christ to be Jehovah, the long-awaited Jewish Messiah, "Immanuel, God with us" (Isaiah 7:14). This is the truth; this is eternal life (1 John 5:20).

David knew the destination was an eternal, joyful life. He finished his thought, "Thou wilt show me the path of life; in thy presence is fullness of joy." Despite feeling alone, confused, or lost in the world, the traveler knew the destination and trusted Jehovah for the journey.

Help us remember the destination, Lord, and trust You on the path.

Living the Faith Life

And the Lord said unto Moses, "Is the Lord's hand waxed short?
Thou shalt see now whether My word shall
come to pass unto thee or not."
—Numbers 11:23

The Lord has given us every kind of promise about His faithfulness to us personally. He has clearly proclaimed that with Him all things are possible. He has declared Himself to be our Shepherd, leading us into righteousness, protecting us from evil, supplying our "green pastures." Yet, like Moses, we doubt Him; we continue to whine, complain, question, and agonize.

Moses had seen the Lord do miracles. He had witnessed the pillar of fire leading the Israelites; he had experienced the daily supply of manna; he had seen the angel of death pass over the homes of the Israelites in Egypt. He had visibly had God's glory settle on him. Yet when the Lord said He would supply fresh meat for perhaps two to three million Israelites, Moses told the Lord it was impossible (Numbers 11:21-22).

What about you? God has promised to supply our needs. Yet when we see that our situation is hopeless, we give up on His faithfulness. We, of course, are looking at the sufficiency (or lack of sufficiency) in the visible realm and help is not on the way. In fact, from our perspective, it is often too late. We have reached a place financially, emotionally, physically where our circumstances are now truly hopeless. We have now fully indulged in unbelief.

Charles Spurgeon, the great English preacher, wrote, "The ground of faith is not the sufficiency of the visible means for the performance of God's promises, but rather the all-sufficiency of the invisible God, who will most surely do as He hath said He would."

The life of faith is the life the Lord is constantly teaching us to live while we are here on earth. The ultimate life of faith would be living with no hopes placed in our visible circumstances or in the creature comforts or in human supply, including our own capability and self-effort. We would be, every moment, saying with King David, "My soul, wait thou only upon God; for my expectation is from Him. He only is my rock and my salvation" (Psalm 62:5-6).

However, we are learning to live by faith. Perhaps we need to embrace our current situations as gifts from Him. His purpose is being accomplished in us. We are being trained to learn to walk, not by sight, but by faith in His faithfulness.

Father, help us believe that Your Word will indeed come to pass and to know that Your promises are to be relied upon in every circumstance.

No Favoritism

For there is no respect of persons with God.
—Romans 2:11

The world has a measuring stick for almost every category of living. For example, it is better to be rich than poor. It is better to be attractive than unattractive. Good grades get accolades; bad grades don't. This carries over into spiritual "measuring sticks." Famous Christians or "gifted" Christians must be more valuable than nobodies. People who give lots of money to the church or to missions must be more loved by God. The more Bible verses you know, the more God must bless you. The less you pray, the less God loves you. The more obedient you are, the more God respects and loves you. Does any of this sound familiar to you?

The Jewish leaders of the first century believed that this was exactly the way God worked. The more laws the Pharisees kept, the more verses they memorized, the more they kept themselves "separate" from the unclean, pagan Gentiles, the more they thought God favored them and would give them a place of honor in His kingdom.

The Scripture teaches the very opposite. God told Samuel, the prophet, that David, the young shepherd boy, was to be king. "The Lord does not look at the things man looks at. Man looks at the outward appearance, but the Lord looks at the heart" (1 Samuel 16:7 NIV).

As Paul wrote in Romans, "For God does not show favoritism" (Romans 2:11 NIV). Here he taught the truth that the Lord loves pagan Gentiles who believe, just as He loves law-keeping Pharisees who come to Him by faith. The actual Greek word behind this English word favoritism is *prosopolepsia*; God has no acceptance of faces i.e., our outward performance or good works.

Peter discovered this truth when he was called to share the gospel of the grace of God with Cornelius, a Roman centurion who was not a religious Jew. "Then Peter began to speak: 'I now realize how true it is that God does not show favoritism....'" The circumcised believers [religious Jews] who had come with Peter were astonished that the gift of the Holy Spirit had been poured out even on the Gentiles (Acts 10:34, 45 NIV).

How might this truth (that God does not accept faces) encourage us as believers? Perhaps it helps to recognize the Lord looks at our hearts, not our faces. Rather than evaluating our lives by our performance or our efforts, we need to examine our heart condition.

The Lord said, "Blessed are the pure in heart for they shall see God" (Matthew 5:8). "Out of the abundance of the heart the mouth speaketh. A good man out of the good treasure of his heart brings forth good things.... For by thy words thou shalt be justified, and by thy words thou shalt be condemned" (Matthew 12:34-35, 37).

What does it mean to be "pure in heart"? What does it mean that we will be judged by our words? Remember that Jeremiah the prophet told us, "The heart is desperately wicked..." (Jeremiah 17:9).

The key to understanding these Scriptures is found in Ezekiel and in Romans. Ezekiel told us that the Lord Himself has to create a new heart in us. "A new heart also will I give you" (Ezekiel 36:26). And when God gives us a new heart, a transformation occurs. "For if you tell others with your own mouth that Jesus Christ is your Lord, and believe in your own heart that God raised him from the dead, you will be saved. For it is with your heart that you believe and are justified; and it is with your mouth that you confess and are saved" (Romans 10:9-10 LB). Our hearts are made pure by believing in Christ's death and resurrection and the Lord Himself has to give us the gift of faith and create the new heart before we can believe. "No one can say, 'Jesus is Lord,' except by the Holy Spirit" (1 Corinthians 12:3 NIV).

Again, how might we be encouraged by knowing that God is no respecter of persons, that He doesn't "accept faces?" We can know that He alone is good; He alone is truly rich; He alone is the One Who ordains our gifts and talents; He alone calls us, individually, to serve in the precise way and place that fulfills His purposes.

For example, the thief on the cross believed in his heart just moments before he died. Yet he is of equal value and equally loved in heaven as the disciples whom Jesus called, who healed the sick and were, in some cases, martyred for their faith. How can this be? Because God is love; His plan is perfect; and He has ordained what our assignment on earth will be (Ephesians 1:11, 2:10).

These truths bring freedom, liberty, and peace into our lives as we meditate on them. We can give up "striving" to be more spiritual; we can give up measuring our lives against someone else's life; we can let go of envy and jealousy; we can quit focusing on our failures; we can let go of pride and self-righteousness and judging others. Why? Because all that is important to the Lord is the condition of our hearts. And He alone can change hearts.

Lord, help us not to focus on faces, even our own face. Rather, "Let Your light shine in our hearts to give us the light of the knowledge of the glory of God in the face of Christ" (2 Corinthians 4:6 NIV).

Life Eternal: To Know God

And this is life eternal, that they might know Thee,
the only true God, and Jesus Christ, whom Thou hast sent.
—John 17:3

The Savior, in His prayer to the Father in John 17, makes it very clear that "the way to have eternal life" is to know the Father and His Son (John 17:3 NLT). An interesting question is: What does it mean to know God? If we had asked Saul the Pharisee, a Jewish leader who knew the Torah and worshipped God, "Saul, do you know God?" his answer would have been a resounding "Yes, of course!"

Yet it was this very religious, Bible-teaching, law-keeping Saul who was confronted by God Himself on the road to Damascus. And the very question Saul asked was, "Who art Thou, Lord?" (Acts 9:5). Saul did not know God. He was simply following a religious belief system.

The apostle Philip, one of the first disciples to be called, walked with Jesus for three years, listened to Him teach, even brought others to hear the Lord (John 1:44-51). Yet it was Philip who said, "Lord, show us the Father and we will be satisfied" (John 14:8 NLT). The Lord answered, "Philip, don't you even yet know who I am, even after all the time I have been with you? Anyone who has seen me has seen the Father" (John 14:7 NLT).

What does it mean to know God? The Greek language provides some helpful insight. Two primary words are translated as *know* in the New Testament. They are *ginosko* and *oida*. The latter, *oida*, is a subjective, intuitive awareness that involves no real focus. For example, we know the sun will rise in the morning, though we might be hard pressed to explain it astronomically. What we know in this sense lacks reflection or any real effort.

The word *ginosko* is an objective knowing. It means to have acquired knowledge by firsthand experience. This kind of knowing involves a sense of focus, true attention that results in grasping an in-depth understanding. In John 17:3 Jesus uses the verb *ginosko* when He says that the way to eternal life is to know the Father and the Son. There is a deep sense of intimacy in this kind of knowing. When we read that Joseph "knew" not Mary, the word *ginosko* is used.

Once Saul the Pharisee truly came to know God, his entire relationship with his Creator changed. Saul became Paul; he now knew the name of God. When he asked, "Who are you?" Jesus answered, "I am Jesus whom thou persecutest" (Acts 9:5). He experienced a firsthand encounter with the Lord!

Doubting Thomas, who also had "known" the Lord for three years, finally touched the resurrected Christ and suddenly truly

187

knew Him. The Lord invited Thomas to come close and place his hands on His wounds. Thomas, at that moment, knew Him. He exclaimed, "My Lord and My God" (John 20:28). He had entered into an intimate knowledge of the Savior.

Perhaps one of the most significant truths for us is found in Philippians 3:10. The apostle Paul had known the Lord for more than twenty years when he wrote this letter from his prison in Rome. He said that nothing else mattered in his life except "that I might know [*ginosko*] Him, and the power of His resurrection, and the fellowship of His sufferings, being made conformable unto His death."

What a calling! What a goal! What a focus! What a worthy endeavor—to know the infinite One. We will never plumb the depths, but we can ask for greater revelation from the Spirit Who dwells in us. The apostle Paul remained focused, every hour of every day, on knowing Him more fully.

Lord, we want to know You intimately and have a personal relationship with You that involves a deep and true comprehension of Who You really are.

When the Lord Doesn't Answer

I called Him, but He gave me no answer.
—Song of Solomon 5:6

One of our greatest "faith testers" is to ask the Lord for help, call out to Him for relief, or long for a sense of His love and presence…and receive no answer. The result of the Lord's seeming silence in our lives is often depression, hopelessness, frustration, or even a feeling of our own "unworthiness" as the reason for His lack of response.

However, the fact is: the Lord does hear our prayers! As C. H. Spurgeon wrote, "God keeps a file of our prayers…they are treasured in the King's archives." David, the psalmist, who had so many severe testings of his faith wrote, "You record my wanderings; put my tears in Thy bottle…" (Psalm 56:8). King David had confidence in the fact that the Lord was keeping a loving eye on all his trials and was lovingly valuing every agonizing tear

David shed. He survived his worst moments because he knew, by faith, that God had His hand of love and mercy on him, in spite of the critical circumstances David faced.

It seems that one of the methods the Lord uses to expand our faith is to test us—allow experiences or situations in our lives that may appear desperate, even hopeless, to us. The agony of the patriarch Job is the classic example of this. Job was a true saint, mature in his faith, a wonderful man of God, a caring father and husband. The Scripture tells us Job was "perfect and upright," one who feared God and shunned evil (Job 1:1). Yet the Lord gave Satan permission to test this saint to the utmost. Nevertheless, at the end of this saga we read, "So the Lord blessed the latter end of Job more than his beginning" (Job 42:12).

Some of our unanswered questions in the midst of trials are "Why, Lord? What's the point? Couldn't You just give us a simple answer? Why these painful, uncomfortable circumstances?"

This side of heaven we may not know the answers to these questions. But we have been given some clues as to why God uses this faith-building method. Faith is about believing what cannot be seen. Saints are those who demonstrate the reality of Christ's existence by walking through agonizing human circumstances with peace and joy because our trust, knowledge, and understanding are based on what we know to be true in the invisible realm. Thus, we are lighting the way to saving faith for those who have not yet come to Christ.

But we must learn how to see the invisible ourselves before we are lighthouses of peace and joy. We are taught, by the Lord's sovereign hand, how to become "partakers of His divine nature

by having to rely on His exceeding great and precious promises"
(2 Peter 1:4).

*Lord, help us embrace our circumstances as Your means for
enhancing Your light in and through us, helping darkened eyes see
into the invisible realm by faith.*

Signposts
to the Savior

*The only sign I will give them is the sign of the
prophet Jonah. For as Jonah was in the belly of
the great fish three days and three nights, so I,
the Son of Man, will be in the heart of the earth
for three days and three nights.*
—Matthew 12:39b-40 NLT

The Creator Shakes His Creation

For thus saith the Lord of hosts:
Yet once, it is a little while, and I will shake the heavens,
and the earth, and the sea, and the dry land.
And I will shake all nations,
and the desire of all nations shall come....
—*Haggai 2:6-7*

As we watched in horror the ravages of the earthquake and tsunami in Southeast Asia, we were sobered by the reality of the sovereignty of God over His creation.

The news reported that more than twelve nations were physically shaken in this 2004 event. The earth's rotation was disrupted; islands were displaced into new locations; this event was described as "an unprecedented catastrophe."

Yet I wonder how many recognize the voice of God calling for His lost sheep through these and similar events? The Creator speaks through His creation. In the world today we have come to dismiss natural catastrophes or meteorological events as simply the work of "Mother Nature." Or a scientific explanation is given as the reason for these occurrences.

Yet the Scripture tells us that God often uses natural disasters as a judgment upon evil in the world. It was the Lord Who said to Noah, "Look! I am about to cover the earth with a flood that will destroy every living thing. Everything on earth will die" (Genesis 6:17 NLT).

The Lord often demonstrates His presence through earthquakes. The crucifixion of Christ was one of those moments. "He gave up his spirit. At that moment…the earth shook, rocks split apart, and tombs opened" (Matthew 27:51-52 NLT).

At the resurrection of Christ the Scripture records, "Early on Sunday morning…suddenly there was a great earthquake, because an angel of the Lord came down from heaven" (Matthew 28:1-3 NLT). When Christ returns there will be a major earthquake, and the Mount of Olives will split in half (Zechariah 4:3-5 NLT).

The Lord Himself has told us what the signs of His return will include. "Nations and kingdoms will proclaim war against each other, and there will be earthquakes in many parts of the world, and famine. But all this will be only the beginning of the horrors to come. But when these things begin to happen, watch out" (Mark 13:8-9 NLT).

Many of the skeptics say that there have always been these natural events. The apostle Peter wrote about these very skeptics, "In the last days there will be scoffers who will laugh at the truth…. They will question the promise Jesus made to return. They will say, 'Why, as far back as anyone can remember everything has remained exactly the same…'" (2 Peter 3:3-4 NLT).

In response Peter said, "They deliberately forget that God made the heavens by the word of his command, and he brought the earth up from the water and surrounded it with water. Then he used the water to destroy the world with a mighty flood. And God has also commanded that the heavens and the earth will be consumed by fire on the day of judgment, when ungodly people will perish" (2 Peter 3:5-7 NLT).

The prophet Isaiah described the Lord's coming in these words. "The Lord will march forth like a mighty man…full of fury. He will say, 'I have restrained myself. But now I will give full vent to my fury…. I will level the mountains and the hills….'" (Isaiah 42:12-15 NLT).

Isaiah also wrote, "In an instant, I, the Lord Almighty, will come against them with thunder and earthquake and great noise, with whirlwind and storm and consuming fire" (Isaiah 29:6 NLT). And, again, Isaiah quotes the Lord, "I am the Lord; there is no other God…. I am the one who sends good times and bad times…. Destruction is certain for those who argue with their Creator" (Isaiah 45:5-10 NLT).

The Lord Himself told us how we are to respond in the midst of this earthly turmoil. "When all these things begin to happen, stand straight and look up, for your salvation is near" (Luke 21:28 NLT).

Lord, give us eyes to see You in every aspect of the circumstances and events unfolding in the visible world.

Cain and Abel - Man's Way or God's Way

Abel was a keeper of sheep.
—Genesis 4:2

The Old Testament is constantly pointing us to Christ Jesus. Every story, every event, even the very geographical locations are signposts to the Savior, heavenly treasures in the Word. Jesus Himself always taught the gospel from the Old Testament Scripture. "And beginning at Moses and all the prophets, he expounded unto them, in all the scriptures, the things concerning Himself" (Luke 24:27).

Cain and Abel, the sons of Adam and Eve, were no doubt both instructed in the Word of God by their parents. Adam and Eve had learned the gospel as it is given in Genesis 3:15. They had both come to know that sin is covered only by the shedding of blood based on the fact that the Lord covered them in coats of skin.

However, when Cain came to worship the Lord, he brought "the fruit of the ground" (Genesis 4:3). Yet the ground had just been cursed by God (Genesis 3:17). The fruit of this cursed ground was Cain's offering, the fruit of his own hard work in the field.

Abel, in contrast, was a shepherd, a keeper of the sheep. He apparently understood that sin could only be covered through a blood sacrifice. He brought his finest lamb as his offering. God honored Abel's sacrifice but did not accept Cain's offering. Cain, in his anger, killed his brother.

Our Great Shepherd, the keeper of the sheep, came as the Lamb of God and offered Himself as the perfect blood sacrifice to cover and atone for our sins. Yet His own Jewish brothers and sisters participated in His murder. And the religious leaders of the day, proud of the works of their own hands, did not want to hear the gospel. They did not want a Messiah Who would die. They did not believe they were sinners. They did not respond to the voice of the Shepherd.

The Lord Himself confronted Cain concerning his actions (Genesis 4:9). Cain denied his guilt, much like the Pharisees and scribes did. Then the Lord said, "The voice of your brother's blood cries unto Me from the ground" (Genesis 4:10). Abel's blood served as condemnation for Cain.

Amazingly, Jesus Himself underscores the significance of Abel's shed blood. He speaks to the religious leaders of the first century and explains that they, like Cain, will be counted as fugitives from heaven. They have rejected God's plan of salvation. The "righteous blood" of Abel will cry out from the ground against them because Abel was a foreshadowing of the righteous blood of Christ Himself (Matthew 23:33-36).

May we remember that the voice of our Shepherd, the Keeper of the sheep, cries out on our behalf every day because His righteous blood covers our sin. We have believed, by faith, in the message from above, which says that "without the shedding of blood there is no forgiveness of sin" (Hebrews 9:22). Oh, what a Shepherd Who has given His life for the sheep.

The Carpenter: Builder of Heaven and Earth

Is not this the carpenter, the son of Mary...?
—Mark 6:3

During His days on earth the Lord earned His daily bread through carpentry. Often, when the unbelieving religious leaders heard this Carpenter teaching the Scriptures or saw Him heal the sick, they were undone by the strangeness of it all. They demeaned Him by reminding the onlookers that Jesus was simply a local tradesman, a nobody, a lowly carpenter.

But what an amazing treasure is hidden in this hurled epithet. Jesus Christ is, indeed, the Carpenter. The Greek word for carpenter is *tekton,* which means builder or constructor.

In Hebrews 11:10 we read that Abraham looked for the city "whose builder and maker is God." The Greek word for builder is *technites,* formed from the same root word as *tekton.* God is a *tekton.* He is a carpenter. He is the Carpenter. Isn't it interesting that when He became visible, in His incarnate body, He came as a carpenter? He was revealing His majesty as the Builder of the heavens and the earth.

In the only other New Testament passage that refers to Jesus' trade, the crowd taunts, "Is not this the carpenter's son...?" (Matthew 13:15). Yes, Joseph, too, serving as Jesus' earthly father, was also a carpenter. Yet hidden in these words is another amazing message. God, the heavenly Father of Jesus, the Son, is also a carpenter, for they are One. The Son is the image of the Father.

The Greek word for builder (*technites*) can also be translated architect or designer. Our Lord is an Artist. He is the most gifted Artist Who has ever created! And we are the work of His hands. David, the psalmist, writes, "Thank you for making me so wonderfully complex! Your workmanship is marvelous.... You watched me as I was being formed in utter seclusion, as I was woven together in the dark of the womb" (Psalm 139:14-15 NLT). Another translation of woven is skillfully embroidered.

You and I are His unique creations. In Ephesians 2:10 Paul wrote, "For we are God's masterpiece, He has created us anew in Christ Jesus so that we can do the good things he planned for us long ago." The Greek word for masterpiece is *poema*, from which we get poem, a work of art.

Great architects and designers begin with a plan. They create what they have designed to serve a specific purpose.

Lord, help us see each day the purpose for which You have uniquely designed and embroidered us.

Knowing Your Bible Won't Get You to Heaven

Christ died for our sins, according to the Scriptures....
—1 Corinthians 15:3

The only Scripture in the first century was the Old Testament. And virtually the entire Jewish community was familiar with this written Word of God. These scrolls had been available to them for centuries. The rabbis taught from them in the synagogues.

Trained and educated as a Pharisee, Saul (who later became Paul, the great apostle to the Gentiles) knew the Scripture. As a Pharisee he was required to memorize the entire Torah, the first five books of the Old Testament. Yet Saul did not recognize Jesus as the Messiah. He was murdering the Christians in the years following the resurrection of Christ. Saul knew his Bible, but he had missed the message.

As a Jew, Saul knew that the Feast of the Passover celebrated the slaying of a lamb whose blood, spattered on the wood of each home, would protect those within from the angel of death. The destroyer would "pass over" those covered with the blood of a lamb (Exodus 12). Saul had probably heard John the Baptist proclaim Jesus to be the long-awaited Lamb without blemish Whose blood must be shed for protection from God's judgment on sin.

Saul knew that Isaiah, the most famous of the Old Testament prophets, had described the Messiah as One Who would be "wounded for our transgressions" and Who would die innocently as "an offering for sin" (Isaiah 53).

He knew the significance of the life of the prophet Jonah. Jonah was understood to be a picture of the coming Messiah, Who would be "buried three days and three nights" and be restored to proclaim salvation to all who would believe.

Saul also knew Isaiah had written that the Messiah would be born of a virgin (Isaiah 7:14); He would be God in the flesh, Immanuel, God with us (Isaiah 9:6). Saul knew this King would be born in Bethlehem (Micah 5:2). In addition, he knew the great Messianic psalm of David's in which the rejection of the Messiah and His crucifixion are described in graphic detail (Psalm 22).

Yet Saul did not recognize Jesus Christ to be the One Whom the Father had sent. Only when the Lord Himself came to Saul personally and called him by name did he understand the truth (Acts 9:3-6). Then, and only then, was Saul transformed by the "hearing of the Word." He became Paul, man of God, called to carry the good news to the entire Gentile world of his day.

Oh, the mystery of salvation! Jesus said, "No man can come unto me, except it were given unto him of my Father" (John 6:65). The Spirit Himself must reveal the Son to us and call us by name. For we are "dead in trespasses and sin." He alone brings life. Without this gift of life we cannot hear His call or understand His written Word.

Oh Lord, in these last days when scoffers abound, open our eyes that we might see. Anoint Your Word in our hearts. May we see Your "blood on the wood" and know You shed it willingly for us, Your sheep, whom You call by name according to the Scriptures.

He was Crushed for our Sake

Then cometh Jesus with them unto a place called Gethsemane.
—Matthew 26:36

Jesus went to a place called "the olive press." That is the actual translation from the Hebrew for the word *Gethsemane*. This was an olive grove, the place where the olives were crushed to release precious oil. This treasured oil was the source of light in virtually every home.

And it is in Gethsemane that the crushing of the Messiah begins. The Hebrew word for crushed is *daka*. It is the same word translated as "bruised" in Isaiah 53:10. "Yet it pleased the Lord to bruise Him…." And in Isaiah 53:5 we read "He was bruised for our iniquities." The Father crushed His only begotten Son so that we could be delivered "from the power of darkness and translated into the kingdom of His dear Son, in whom we have redemption through his blood, even the forgiveness of sins" (Colossians 1:13-14). We have been translated into the light.

There was another "bruising" being carried out in that same garden. In Genesis 3:15 the Lord speaks to the serpent and says, "The seed of the woman" (the Messiah) will "bruise your head and you shall bruise his heel." It was in Gethsemane that a seed of Satan, Judas Iscariot, betrayed the Seed of the woman and the Messiah was crushed. But the Savior survived the death blow Satan thought would be final. The Lord's death and resurrection created what will be the final crushing of the seed of the serpent.

The serpent brought death into the world in the garden of Eden by rebelling against God's plan. Christ brought life into the world in the garden of Gethsemane by submitting to God's plan.

Because we live in time and space, we have yet to fully comprehend what has been accomplished in the heavenlies. Christ spoke from the cross, "It is finished." The death blow, the fatal head wound, has been delivered to Satan and his angels. Death has been defeated. But the end of the drama is not yet visible.

The apostle Paul told us that Christ will eventually put all enemies under His feet. The last enemy to be destroyed is death (1 Corinthians 15:24-25). Paul encouraged the suffering saints in Rome with these words, "And the God of peace shall bruise Satan under your feet shortly" (Romans 16:20).

The olives were crushed by stomping of feet. The enemy will be the one who receives the ultimate crushing. God has promised to make all enemies of the Son His footstool (Psalm 110:1).

Lord, our hearts overflow with gratitude and adoration at Your willingness to receive the crushing in order that we might be freed from the penalty of sin and live eternally with You in the heavenlies. Even so, come quickly, Lord Jesus.

The Tree of Life and the Tree of Death

Who his own self bare our sins in his
own body on the tree....
—1 Peter 2:24

The Hebrew word for tree (*ets*) is also the word for wood or timber. In the garden of Eden we find two important trees, the tree of life and the tree of the knowledge of good and evil (Genesis 2:9). The fruit of the second tree was sin which produced death. Eve, and then Adam, ate from the tree of death. One tree dispensed life; the other dispensed sin.

Gruesome reminders of the punishment for sin abound in the Old Testament. The Pharaoh's chief baker was "hanged on a tree" (Genesis 40:19). Evil Haman in the book of Esther was "hanged on the gallows," the wood of the tree. And so it is written, "Cursed is everyone who is hung on a tree" (Deuteronomy 21:23; Galatians 3:13 NLT).

We begin to grasp the significance of Peter's words when he said that Christ was hung on a tree, cursed by God, because He bore our sins. "He who knew no sin became sin for us that we might be made the righteousness of God in Him" (2 Corinthians 5:21).

The Lord was hung on the tree of death and He transformed it into the tree of life for us. When we now eat of Him, the Tree of Life, we have victory over the fruits of sin and death.

Even as the Lord hung on the tree, there were two other "trees" present. Each one had a thief hanging on it, under the curse of death because of his sin. One thief chose not to come to the Tree of Life. He died, cursed. The other thief cried out for forgiveness; he ate of the Tree of Righteousness and received eternal life.

Another significant tree is found in Luke 22:3, at the scene of the Last Supper, where we read, "Then Satan entered into Judas Iscariot." And when Judas later realized that his betrayal would cost Jesus His life, Judas "went out and hanged himself" (Matthew 27:5). The Son of God hung on the tree and the result was life. The son of perdition hung on a tree and the result was death. "For the wages of sin is death, but the free gift of God is eternal life through Christ Jesus our Lord" (Romans 6:23).

As the book of Genesis opened with the tree of life in a garden, so the Lord closes His written Word with the tree of life. In the last chapter of the Bible we see the heavenly city of Jerusalem with the tree of life in a garden. (Interestingly, here the Greek word for tree is *xulon,* which means "living wood.") And we read, "There shall be no more curse" (Revelation 22:3).

Oh Lord, how we praise You for hanging upon the tree in our place and exchanging our sin for Your righteousness. May we fall down in adoration and continual praise!

Peace and Safety are Ours

He was beaten that we might have peace.
He was whipped, and we were healed!
—Isaiah 53:5 NLT

Christ died for our sins, was buried, and rose again on the third day. That is the means of our salvation. Our Lord died in our place. He paid for our sins. Most of us feel secure in our salvation because we have believed this truth.

However, do we fully understand and appreciate all His death provides for us? "He was beaten that we might have peace." In the King James Version we read, "The chastisement of our peace was on Him." One of the major fears or anxieties in the heart of believers is the sense that God is not happy with us. We are quite aware of our sins and shortcomings. And we have a vague concern, if not a paralyzing fear, of what God will do to us because of our failures.

Yet in this verse we see that the Lord took upon Himself the "chastisement," the heavy hand of God that would have been laid upon us as sinners. He stood in our place so that we might never have to receive or be worried about receiving this form of God's response to sin. Thus the Lord provided peace for us. Perhaps in praising Him for this peace that is ours, we will experience a greater awareness of this incredible gift. Peace. It is ours because of His being chastised in our place.

And then we read, "He was whipped, and we were healed." The Hebrew word for whipped or stripes is *chaburah* and it means bruises and scars. The Lord received bruising and scarring on our behalf. Why? Because God hates sin. Mysteriously, the Lord reached down through the ages and lifted our individual sins, all of them, off of us and onto Himself. Our Lord Jesus experienced the horrific lashing, in addition to the agony of the cross itself, so that we will never be whipped.

What does the Scripture say is the gift to us? "By His stripes we are healed." The Hebrew word for healed is *rapha*. Significantly, one of the names of God is Jehovah-Rapha, the One Who heals and makes whole. In Psalm 23:3 we read that "He restores our soul." The name of God used there is Jehovah the Healer. He restores us to wholeness in our souls by His stripes. We are no longer broken, scarred people if we are in Christ. The Father now sees us as whole, perfect, righteous, and restored to complete wellness spiritually.

The apostle Peter must have lived with great self-condemnation and spiritual self-flagellation. Yet his comfort was in this very work of Christ. Christ was flagellated, whipped, so Peter (and we) might let go of our own self-flagellation. Peter wrote, speaking of Christ, "Who of his own self bore our sins in his own body on the tree…by whose stripes ye were healed. For ye were as sheep going astray; but are now returned unto the Shepherd and Bishop of your souls" (1 Peter 2:24-25).

Lord Jesus, we give You endless praise for the peace and wholeness that is ours because Your body was scarred and broken on our behalf. Help us to see this incredible truth.

Thorns:
A Sign of God's Curse

Then came Jesus forth, wearing the crown of thorns....
—John 19:5

Jesus told the disciples that mockery would accompany His death. The Son of Man, He said, shall be delivered to "the Gentiles to mock, and to scourge and to crucify" (Matthew 20:19).

It is not surprising that one of the wicked instruments Satan used in this mockery was the painful crown of thorns. In Genesis 3:17-18 we discover that thorns are a result and a visible reminder of God's curse on sin. "Cursed is the ground...thorns and thistles shall it bring forth to thee."

Christ is the Head of the Body (the believers for whom He died). He took the curse of sin upon His head so that the curse would not fall upon His body. The crown of thorns signals this truth to us.

When the Lord spoke of His coming death, He said He would provide the Jews with one sign and one sign only, the sign of Jonah. "For as Jonah was three days and three nights in the whale's belly; so shall the Son of man be three days and three nights in the heart of the earth" (Matthew 12:39-40). (It is significant to note that Christ believed Jonah's experience to be a literal one, just as His own would be.)

When we read of Jonah's experience we discover he actually died inside the great fish. He descended into Sheol, the place of the dead, with weeds wrapped around his head! "I cried... unto the Lord out of the belly of hell (Sheol)...the weeds were wrapped about my head...the earth with her bars was about me forever" (Jonah 2:2, 5-6). Jonah was a sign, complete with a crown of "thorns!"

The Lord spoke to the fish and Jonah was resurrected, delivered to high ground by the Word of God. The curse, which results in death, was removed from Jonah because he cried out to the Lord for help as he was dying, having recognized his own rebellion.

As believers we have been delivered from death, from the curse of sin, by the "hearing of the Word." In Matthew 13 Jesus uses the parable of the sower to illustrate this. He teaches that the seed that falls on ground that is under the curse of sin will be choked out by thorns. The Greek word for thorn here is *akantha*, the same word used to describe the crown of thorns. Yet the seed that falls on good ground springs up and bears fruit. Good ground is soil that has had the curse removed so it can receive the seed.

Jesus provides the explanation of His parable. He says the sower of the good seed is the Son of Man, the ground is the world, and the seed is the Word of God (Matthew 13:18-23, 37-38). The "good ground" represents the person who hears His Word and understands it.

It is significant that "faith comes by hearing and hearing by the Word of God" (Romans 10:17). In order for the seed (the Word of God) to take root and bear fruit, the thorns have to be removed. The "good ground" had to be prepared by the Sower Himself. The One Who removed the curse of sin from us by taking the curse on His own head is also the One Who removes the rebellion (thorns) in our own hearts so we can be translated out of the kingdom of darkness into the kingdom of light by faith.

The Word of God became flesh and dwelt among us. He wore the crown of thorns so that we can wear the crown of life through faith in His death and resurrection on our behalf. What a Savior!

Oh how we praise You, Lord, as the One Who has saved us from the curse of eternal death. You hung on the tree of death so that we may eat from the tree of life eternally.

The Scriptural Significance of Clothes

After they had nailed him to the cross,
the soldiers gambled for his clothes....
—Matthew 27:35 NLT

The soldiers had no idea of the significance of these clothes, the clothes of the King of righteousness.

In Genesis the Lord teaches us the significance of clothing. After Adam and Eve sinned "they suddenly felt shame at their nakedness. So they strung fig leaves together around their hips to cover themselves" (Genesis 3:7 NLT).

The Lord God taught them that their attempt at clothing themselves to cover up their shame (sin) was inadequate. He Himself shed blood in the garden and "made clothing from animal skins for Adam and his wife" (Genesis 3:21 NLT).

The prophet Isaiah recognized the message God was sending in the garden. He wrote, "We are all infected and impure with sin. When we proudly display our righteous deeds, we find they are but filthy rags" (Isaiah 64:6 NLT).

Zechariah, another Old Testament prophet, reinforced this biblical message. He described a vision of an earthly priest standing in a heavenly court. He wrote, "Jeshua's clothing was filthy. So the angel said, 'Take off his filthy clothes.' Then He said to Jeshua, 'See I have taken away your sins, and now I am giving you these fine new clothes'" (Zechariah 3:3-4 NLT).

The prophet Daniel saw the Lord Himself. He saw the Ancient One sit down to judge all men. "His clothing was as white as snow, his hair like whitest wool (Daniel 7:9 NLT).

The apostle John saw the Lord in the heavenlies also. "And standing in the middle...was the Son of Man. He was wearing a long robe...His head and hair were white like wool, as white as snow" (Revelation 1:13, 24 NLT). Then the Lord tells the churchgoers in Sardis that He will never erase their names from the Book of Life if they are clothed in white (Revelation 3:5).

Christ, as the second Adam, became sin for us (2 Corinthians 5:21). Thus He hung naked on the cross, just as Adam found himself naked in the garden. (A Jewish man without a full undergarment on was counted as naked.) He did this so we could be clothed in white, the garment of His righteousness (2 Corinthians 5:21).

As the soldiers at the foot of the cross gambled for the Lord's earthly clothing, just above their heads, cleansing blood was being poured out for sin—the blood that could provide eternal clothing for them. The blood that, though their sins were "as scarlet, they shall be white as snow" (Isaiah 1:18). They missed the significant message. They were preoccupied with the visible, the events of this world.

Lord, help us not to be distracted with the visible when what You have provided for us is to be experienced in the invisible realm of Your kingdom. May we look to Your cleansing blood and walk in the heavenly garments of Your righteousness.

Good Results
from the Worst Calamities

She called his name Ben-oni (son of sorrow),
but his father called him Benjamin (son of my right hand).
—Genesis 35:18

This verse comes from the account of Rachel and Jacob. Rachel, the mother of Joseph, died at the birth of her second son. Just as she was leaving this earth "she called his name Ben-oni," which means son of sorrow in Hebrew. She was faced with death, never to be with her beloved Jacob again, never to have the privilege of raising this son.

Yet Jacob, who treasured his wife Rachel, even in his sorrow while standing by her side in this moment, changed this boy's name to Benjamin, "son of my right hand" in Hebrew.

As the Scripture often provides, there is a foreshadowing here of another mother and another Father and their Son. When Mary became pregnant by the Holy Spirit, the Father of the Son, she was told her child would save His people from their sins.

The prophet Isaiah told us that the coming Messiah will be "a man of sorrows, and acquainted with grief." The Lord's mother understood the sorrow that would be hers in the death of her Son. Yet, His Father knew that this Son would serve "at His right hand" for all eternity. "It is Christ that died, yea rather, that is risen again, who is even at the right hand of God, who also maketh intercession for us" (Romans 8:34).

An encouraging truth is hidden in these scriptures. As Charles Spurgeon wrote in his commentary on this account in Genesis, "To every matter there is a bright as well as a dark side.… Faith's way of walking is to cast all care upon the Lord, and then to anticipate good results from the worst calamities…when death itself appears, faith points to the light of resurrection…making our dying Ben-oni to be our living Benjamin."

Surely this is one of our most difficult daily challenges as children of the King–to see His hand of love at work in the darkest, most difficult circumstances. Yet this is the life of faith. If we understood the events that seem tragic or difficult or senseless, we would not need to walk by faith. But the Lord is teaching us to rely on Him, His character, His unchanging love, His perfect plan, and His promise that all the details of our lives are designed for our good and His ultimate glory.

Lord, lift our eyes off that which we see around us. Help us to see into the realm of the invisible where You reign over all.

We are Drawn to Know Christ!

And I, if I be lifted up from the earth,
will draw all men unto me.
—John 12:32

The Lord continuously depicted His crucifixion as His being "lifted up." In John 3:14 He explained, "And as Moses lifted up the serpent in the wilderness, even so must the Son of Man be lifted up." In this passage, Christ refers to the strange truth found in Numbers 21:7-9. There we find sins forgiven in the lives of the Israelites who believed God's Word and looked up, by faith, to the brass serpent on a pole.

This was a picture, or type, of the coming Messiah, Who would "become sin" (the serpent image) and pass through the fire (brass) on behalf of all who would look up to Him by faith.

But there is a greater truth hidden in the Lord's statement, "I will draw all men unto me." Do "all men" come to know and believe in Christ? No. Then what does the Lord mean in this statement?

In this passage the Greek simply reads, "I will draw all unto me." The Lord had explained this truth in an earlier discourse with His disciples. In John 6:37 we read, "All that the Father giveth me shall come to me and him that cometh to me I will in no wise cast out. Christ continued to explain what He meant in John 6:44. "No man can come to me except the Father which hath sent Me, draw him...."

The New Living Translation reads, "However, those the Father has given me will come to me, and I will never reject them.... For people can't come to me unless the Father who sent me draws them to me..." (John 6:37, 44 NLT).

Jesus is saying that when He is lifted up on the cross, all those who have been given to Him as a gift from the Father will come to Him. And the Father will draw them to the Son.

Christ goes on to say, "And this is the will of God, that I should not lose even one of all those He has given me, but that I should raise them to eternal life at the last day" (John 6:39 NLT).

The magnificence of the grace of God is displayed in these amazing truths. First, we are told that the knowledge that Christ died for our sins (was lifted up on the cross) is the spellbinding truth God uses to draw us to the Son. Then we discover that the Father has given us as His own gift to the Son. The sovereign Lord of creation, the Potter, has turned a lump of clay into a bejeweled vessel of honor as a love gift to His Son. That lump of clay is you if you find yourself drawn to Jesus Christ.

And more good news! No one, absolutely no human being on the planet who is drawn to believe in Him will ever be turned away. Why? Because there is nothing in us that qualifies us for eternal life. The basis for our receiving the gift of eternal life is the Father's plan. His plan is to give you, a child of faith, to His Son. And He will accomplish His plan.

Listen to these grace-filled words from the Son as He talks about those "sheep" who are His. "I give them eternal life, and they will never perish. No one will snatch them away from me. For my Father has given them to me, and He is more powerful than anyone else. So, no one will snatch them away from me" (John 10:28-29 NLT).

Father, we are drawn to Your Son. And now we see that You are the Author of the drawing. To think You have created us as love gifts to your beloved Son! We bow in awe at Your throne of grace.

A Bride by Blood Shed

And the Lord God caused a deep sleep to fall upon Adam,
and he slept; and He took one of his ribs,
and closed up the flesh...
and from the rib made He a woman,
and brought her unto the man.
—Genesis 2:21-22

Adam obtained his bride through the shedding of his own blood. How startling it is to see the Lord teaching us of His eternal plan in the very opening pages of His book!

We know that Jesus Christ is called the second Adam. Adam was the first man and his actions brought death to all human beings. Christ became man so that His actions might bring life to all who believe. Paul the apostle wrote, "Adam, the first man, was made from the dust of the earth, while Christ, the second man, came from heaven" (1 Corinthians 15:47 NLT).

God Himself caused Adam to fall into a deep sleep. The Hebrew word for sleep in this passage is *yashen* and, figuratively, is a picture of dying. (An entirely different word for sleep is used, for instance, in Genesis 15:12 when it says "a deep sleep fell upon Abram.")

The Father caused the Son to enter into death so that His Bride could be created. The place of this death was "near a garden..." (John 19:41 NLT). During the death process, the second Adam, like the first Adam, had His side pierced and His blood shed in order for His Bride to join Him.

The first Adam was made of the earth. But his bride was a unique creation. She was not made from the dust of the earth. She was created from Adam's very own flesh and bone. "She is part of my own flesh and bone!" (Genesis 2:23 NLT). Paul wrote of us, the Bride of Christ, "We are members of His body, of his flesh, and of his bones" (Ephesians 5:30).

In Genesis we read that the Lord Himself presented the bride (Eve) to the first Adam. He "brought her" to Adam (Genesis 2:22). In his letter to the Ephesians, Paul, describing the second Adam, wrote, "He gave up his life for her...He did this to present her to himself as a glorious church... (Ephesians 5:25, 27 NLT). The Lord created and presented the bride in both scenarios!

The Bible closes with a scene in a garden with a river, fruit trees, and the tree of life. In the midst of the garden is the Lamb and His Bride. "In the midst...was the tree of life...and there shall be no more curse...and the Spirit and the bride say, come" (Revelation 22:2-3, 17).

If we are in Christ by faith, we are new creations, bone of His bone, flesh of His flesh. We are a part of His Body and will be presented to Him, "not having spot or wrinkle...holy and without blemish" (Ephesians 5:27).

Lord, You have done it all. What a mysterious, glorious, grace-filled plan! And how wonderful of You to give us clues to what You are doing from the beginning to the end of Your Word!

Saved From What?

Salvation is of the Lord.
—Jonah 2:9

The word *salvation* rarely comes up in social gatherings. Have you noticed that? You don't really win friends and influence people by asking them if they have been "saved." Yet "salvation" is the main topic in the Bible.

Why is it that we are pretty comfortable with other biblical terms like love, peace, hope, and joy? But somehow most folks are not comfortable discussing the topic of salvation. There must be a reason for that.

The Hebrew word for salvation provides shocking insight and understanding. The Hebrew word is *yeshuah*. Does that ring any bells for you? The Battle of Jericho was led by Joshua, which is actually Jehoshua, translated as Jesus in the Greek! In other words, salvation, *yeshuah*, actually means "God saves." Thus, Jesus is the Savior; He is a God Who saves people.

The Hebrew word *yeshuah* means to be brought to safety. The Greek word for salvation is *soteris* and means to be brought to safety and made to be sound or healthy, whole. To be saved is to be made safe, to be made sound.

Then comes another question. From what do we need to be saved? Here is where the heart of discomfort lies for most people today. The Bible says that, left to ourselves, we are headed for eternal destruction and the world just doesn't buy that.

Many will talk about Jesus Christ as a great teacher, even as Savior in some general sense. Many of these same people will even say they believe Christ died on the cross. They occasionally go to church, on Easter or Christmas. But the idea that all human beings, left to themselves, are headed for hell? No. That would be far too radical for most sophisticates in the world today.

Perhaps it would be valuable for us to review exactly what the Bible says about the dangerous condition of human beings which requires that we be rescued, brought to safety by the Savior.

Paul reminded us that all humans "have sinned and fall short of the glory of God." In other words, we are under condemnation because we have broken God's laws. The Greek word for condemnation is *krisis,* which means the judgment of God. (And thus we have the English word crisis.)

The Savior Himself describes what that judgment includes. For those of us who do not come to Him, recognizing that we are sinners who need a Savior, Jesus says, "Depart from Me... into everlasting fire...into everlasting punishment" (Matthew 25:41, 46).

Those of us who believe the Word of God and have placed our faith in Christ as Savior have been saved from the wrath of God. Have we really grasped what it means to be safe in Him?

Have we truly praised Him for the fact that He has provided the way out of this path we were on?

It is noteworthy that in Noah's day he preached that God's judgment was coming on the entire world. Safety was to be found only in the ark. But that was not happy conversation at the social gatherings of the day, given the fact that only eight people went into the ark. The Lord Himself said, "As it was in the days of Noah so shall it be also in the days of the Son of Man" (Luke 17:26). The desperate need for safety from destruction is His message to all who will hear.

Oh Lord, give us grace to hear, to believe, and to treasure the rescuing truth of Your Word. "If you confess with your mouth Jesus as Lord and believe in your heart that God has raised Him from the dead, you will be saved" (Romans 10:9).

Heavenly Dew

I will be as the dew unto Israel.
—Hosea 14:5

These words are those of the Lord speaking to the Israelites, who are grieved over their own failures, sins, and lack of faith. And these are His words to every believer, each one of us who longs to experience more of His grace and mercy in the face of our own inadequacies.

It is interesting that the Lord uses the metaphor of dew as a description of what He is to us. Dew is very gentle, arriving almost unseen and certainly unheard. Dew comes in the night, just before dawn. It cannot be seen initially. The Lord tells us that is how He comes to us. In our darkness, quietly, gently, initially unnoticed, He descends upon us in the midst of our circumstances. His presence is a signal that the light is coming!

There is also a mystery and a miracle about dew. How is water gathered up from the earth, brought into the clouds, and poured out as torrential rain or as gentle dew? The moisture in the atmosphere distills into dew. Who can explain it? And so with the Lord. His work is both mysterious and miraculous. It is worth observing that the dew is not to be explained by man's efforts or anything man can do. So is the mystery of the Holy Spirit coming to refresh our spirits.

In Exodus 16:13-15 we discover that manna, the heavenly food that fed the Israelites, came with the dew. When they asked Moses what this was, He answered, "This is the bread which the Lord has given you to eat." The refreshing dew is a heavenly gift. The bread is as well. No wonder Jesus said, "I am the living bread which came down from heaven: if any man eat of this bread he shall live forever" (John 6:51).

The combined presence of the dew (the water) and the manna (the bread of heaven) has another spiritual application. Jesus explained to the woman at the well that He was the living water, the source of everlasting life (John 4:10,14). He also explained to the disciples that "man does not live by bread alone, but by every Word that proceedeth out of the mouth of God" (Matthew 4:4). There is a mysterious truth in the combination of the dew (water) and the manna (the Word of God). Paul wrote that the Lord sanctifies and cleanses His own "with the washing of water by the Word" (Ephesians 5:26).

It has been said that the heavenly dew is the refresher of our spirits. Earthly dew achieves its purpose through its constancy. It is the constant coming of the dew that allows the desert to blossom and trees to bear fruit. The Lord has promised His constancy in our lives. "I will never leave you nor forsake you"

(Hebrews 13:5). It is through the heavenly dew that the Lord removes our barrenness and sustains our lives.

The Scripture calls us to look heavenward for any and all of our needs. His light shines; His water flows down; His dew drops down; the dove descends with peace; the Comforter comes down from above; the wind brings the breath of life; even His purifying fire comes down from heaven (Luke 9:54).

David wrote that the same dew that descended on the icy peaks of Mount Hermon in Israel is the dew that descended on the lower regions, the mountains of Zion (Psalm 133:3).

Help us understand, Lord Jesus, that You Yourself are the dew. "I will be as the dew...." You will refresh us and sustain us forever, whether we are on the mountain top of life or in a lower valley. You remain constant.

The One and Only Sign

You ask for a miraculous sign, but the only sign
I will give is the sign of the prophet Jonah.
—*Matthew 12:39* NLT

You will remember the story well. The prophet Jonah was a believer who was born in Galilee, served the Israelites faithfully, and then became utterly disobedient to the Lord's call. Instead of obeying the Lord's request to go to Nineveh to preach, Jonah headed in the opposite direction. We know what followed. Jonah was chastened through drowning in a raging sea; then he was rescued by a "prepared" fish. He ultimately ended up in Nineveh and a gigantic revival occurred in that Gentile city. Yet Jonah still had a rebellious attitude about some of the Lord's ensuing actions.

Nevertheless, the Lord Himself speaks of Jonah in an amazing, honoring way. He describes Jonah's life as a "miraculous" sign, the "only" sign the Lord would use to reveal His identity to the Jews. (Jonah was in the belly of the fish three days and three nights as the Lord was to be in the belly of the earth three days and three nights. Both died during their ordeal. Jonah was resurrected from the fish's belly as a sign of the Lord's coming resurrection.) The Lord even testified to Jonah's effectiveness as a preacher. He said, "The men of Nineveh shall rise in judgment with this generation and condemn it." The Lord explained to the unbelieving Jews that the Gentile—formerly pagan—Ninevites will be resurrected because they believed as a result of Jonah's preaching.

Isn't it a display of amazing grace that there is never a mention of Jonah's disobedience or his angry attitude? The Lord simply points to the wondrous results that flowed out of the life of a saint. This is the Lord Who said, "I, even I, am he that blots out thy transgressions for my own sake and will not remember your sins" (Isaiah 43:25).

Or what about Abraham's nephew, Lot, who escaped from the judgment poured out on Sodom and Gomorrah? We recall that Lot's actions were not honorable when he offered to give his daughters over for sexual exploitation by the wicked, fornicating men of Sodom (Genesis 19:4-8). The Lord prevented that from happening. Yet later, after Lot and his daughters had been rescued from that city, Lot became drunk and committed incest with his daughters.

In the New Testament, we read that the Lord delivered "righteous Lot" who was vexed by the wickedness of his day. That "righteous man" had his "righteous soul" vexed day after day there. But "the Lord knows how to deliver the godly out of temptation" (2 Peter 2:7-9). Not one word is written to remind us of Lot's sins and failures. Rather, he is described as a righteous saint, a godly man whom the Lord delivered out of a terrible judgment on evil. The Lord arranged for angels to deliver Lot, much like the fish that had been arranged for Jonah in his circumstances (Genesis 19:15-16).

Or what about Rahab, the harlot? Here was a Gentile woman who was a practicing prostitute in the city of Jericho. She hid two Israelite spies who came in to spy out the land. When the King of Jericho asked her where the men were, Rahab lied. She told him they had left town when, in fact, she had hidden them on her own roof (Joshua 2:1-6). Eventually she was miraculously delivered during the attack on Jericho. She married an Israelite (Salmon) and was Ruth's mother-in-law and King David's great great grandmother! In that lineage the Savior was born (Matthew 1:5-16; Luke 3:23-32).

When we read the roll call of the heroes and heroines of faith in the Old Testament, Rahab is listed with the likes of Abraham, Isaac, Jacob, and Moses (Hebrews 11:17-31). Rahab's incredible faith was displayed in her willingness to receive and protect the spies. She "perished not with them that believed not." God's grace was so showered on Rahab's life that she ended up in the hall of fame for the faithful!

What a Savior we have! He delivers "the godly" out of the worst of circumstances by His "prearranged" plans. And His definition of "godly" is those who believe in Jesus Christ as God in the flesh and the only way into God's presence (1 John 4:1-3.) He saves us from the wrath of His eternal judgment. He doesn't even remember our sins. And He carefully designs the ordained means by which we will serve Him, in spite of ourselves. "For we are his workmanship, created in Christ Jesus for the good works which God has ordained for us" (Ephesians 2:10).

We, like Jonah, Lot, and Rahab, are "miraculous signs" that point to the amazing grace of Jesus Christ!

Lord, may we praise You continuously for Your miraculous gift to us…grace abounding.

The Good Fruit

From Me is thy fruit found.
—Hosea 14:8

As believers, we often hear sermons on the importance of "bearing good fruit." Paul told us in Galatians that "works of the flesh include adultery, fornication…hatred…envyings," (Galatians 5:19). In contrast, he wrote, "But the fruit of the Spirit is love, joy, peace…gentleness, goodness" (Galatians 5:22). He exhorted believers to "walk in the Spirit" and "not fulfill the lust of the flesh" (Galatians 5:16). And truly we desire to do exactly what the apostle outlined—live a life full of the fruit of the Spirit.

The question is, "How is this achieved?" How do we know if we are really bringing forth good fruit? Maybe our good works (trying to serve others, trying to love irritating people, trying to not be angry) are purely the result of disciplined flesh. We are trying to be "good Christians" but our hearts may well be unchanged. What is the Scriptural answer to this dilemma?

The foundational truth for fruit bearing begins in the garden of Eden. There we see two kinds of fruit trees: the tree of life in the midst of the garden, and the tree of the knowledge of good and evil (Genesis 2:9). Adam and Eve were given the tree of life to eat from freely; but they were not to eat of the tree of the knowledge of good and evil.

We know that the tree of life is a symbol of Christ Himself, the life who hung on a tree in our behalf. The other tree infected mankind with the lie that we can be like God, knowing how to make good choices, wise enough to differentiate between good and evil. Today the world abounds with secular humanism, the lie that man is basically good and wise and capable of producing good fruit and good works.

Jesus Christ Himself gave us insight into these two trees. He said, "Even so, every good tree brings forth good fruit; but a corrupt tree brings forth evil fruit. A good tree cannot bring forth evil fruit, neither can a corrupt tree bring forth good fruit. Every tree that does not bring forth good fruit will be hewn down and cast into the fire. Wherefore, by their fruits you shall know them" (Matthew 7:17-20).

Let's examine what the Lord is really saying here. Good trees cannot produce evil fruit. Evil trees cannot produce good fruit. The issue at hand is the tree, not the fruit. In other words, an apple tree cannot produce pears. For apples to be present requires the tree be an apple tree. If we tie apples on a pear tree it may look like an apple tree on the outside, but eventually the fruit will rot because it is not gaining life from the source.

The prophet Hosea quoted Jehovah, "From Me is thy fruit found." Jesus taught the same truth in John chapter fifteen. "I am the true Vine...the branch cannot bear fruit of itself except it abide in the vine. I am the Vine, you are the branches. He that abides in Me and I in him, the same bringeth forth much fruit; for without Me you can do nothing" (John 15:1, 4-5).

In other words, if we are in Christ, the good tree, the Vine, we will produce good fruit because the good life is in us. The Holy Spirit is producing His fruit—His nature—in us. The good tree will produce good fruit because that is the kind of tree it is.

Paul gave us insight and encouragement as believers who want to know how to walk in the Spirit, producing good fruit. "Even when we were dead in sin God made us alive in Christ...this is the gift of God, not of works...for we are His workmanship created in Christ Jesus unto good works, which God has before ordained that we should walk in them" (Ephesians 2:5, 8-10).

If we confess with our mouths and believe in our hearts that Jesus Christ is Lord, we are in the Good Tree, the Tree of Eternal Life. In us, this life will bear fruit, the fruit of the Spirit. And He who has begun this good work in us "will perform it" until the day Jesus returns (Philippians 1:6).

Father, we trust Your faithful work in us, looking unto Jesus, the Vine. He has promised that from Him our "fruit will be found." Thank You, Lord.

The Hand of the Lord

*Filled with compassion, the Lord reached
out His hand and touched the man.*
—Mark 1:41

In the opening chapter of Mark we read, "A man with leprosy came to Him and begged Him on his knees, 'If you are willing, you can make me clean'" (Mark 1:40 NIV).

It is worth noting that this man knew his condition; he knew Christ could heal him if He chose to do so; he knew that Christ was worthy to be worshipped (he came on his knees); and he asked to be made clean. He knew Jesus had the power to heal; yet he also knew Christ might not choose to heal him. He simply came, knowing there was no place else he could go! Jesus was his only hope.

Leprosy, in the Scripture, is a symbol of sin. Like sin, it seems insignificant at first, a small single white spot on the skin. But as one writer says, "its consequences are devastating." The disease eventually attacks the limbs and the soft tissue and, without treatment, it is fatal.

Jesus was a Jewish rabbi. Jews were never to touch a leper, according to the Jewish law. This would make them unfit for worship. Yet we read, "Filled with compassion, Jesus reached out His hand and touched the man" (Mark 1:41 NIV). The Greek word for compassion is *spla,* which means to be moved in your insides. The Lord experienced a deep emotion of caring, seeing the heart's desire, the faith, of this leper kneeling before Him.

Christ spoke to this man, "I am willing. Be clean." Instantly the man was cured (Mark 1:41 NIV). There is cleansing power in the Word of God. There is healing power in the Word of God. The Lord touched this leper with love, spoke His Word, and the leper was transformed. In fact, this new man "went out and began…spreading the news." This is surely an appropriate response to being set free from such agony!

Though we may have come to Christ and asked to be forgiven and made alive in Him, we still, as believers, get infected with sin in our daily lives. Often we feel separated from and rejected by the Lord because of our "leprous" condition.

It is good to remember that the Lord looks upon us with compassion. Like the leper, we can kneel before Him and beg Him to free us from our current condition. And He sees our hearts, not our leprosy.

Though we cannot see the Lord's physical hand today, we have His written Word and the indwelling Holy Spirit Who intercedes for us, applying the Lord's healing touch in our lives. The nail scars in Christ's hands remain a testimony to His love, grace, and mercy for those who come by faith, worshipping Him.

Lord, continue to apply Your shed blood in our lives, day by day, that we might be clean. We offer up our hearts, full of thanksgiving.

The Sacrifice of Thanksgiving

And He took a cup of wine and gave thanks to God for it....
And He said to them,
This is my blood, poured out for many....
—Mark 14:23-24 NLT

Let's reflect on the biblical significance of giving thanks. The Greek word for thanks is *euchar*. This is the root word for the Christian term describing the communion table, the Eucharist celebration.

At the Last Supper the Lord offered up thanks (*euchar*) over the cup of wine, which He said represented His shed blood. He was thanking the Father for what the wine represented, His own blood sacrifice, His death on the cross!

In the Old Testament we read, "Let them offer sacrifices of thanksgiving..." (Psalm 107:22 NLT). In Hebrew, the word translated as sacrifice is *zebach,* which means to slaughter. In other words, the deepest meaning of thanksgiving is related to a death, a giving of thanks for a blood sacrifice!

242

In Psalm 116:17 NLT we read the words of King David, "I will offer you a sacrifice of thanksgiving and call on "the name of the Lord." When David called on the Lord's name, he was aware of the element of this deep connection with sacrifice or slaughter, the shedding of blood.

In Romans 12:1 (NLT) the apostle Paul wrote, "And so dear brothers and sisters, I plead with you to give your bodies to God. Let them be a living and holy sacrifice...." The Greek word translated as sacrifice is *thusia* and means slaughtered animal.

The New Testament clearly teaches us that we died with Christ on the cross. "The law no longer holds you in its power, because you died to its power when you died with Christ on the cross" (Romans 7:4 NLT). In Galatians we read, "I have been crucified with Christ. I myself no longer live, but Christ lives in me. So I live my life in this earthly body by trusting in the Son of God, who loved me and gave himself for me" (Galatians 2:19-20 NLT).

The heart of true thanksgiving is an awareness that the ultimate slaughter has occurred. Christ shed His blood in our behalf and He thanked His Father for the privilege of going to be slaughtered, to die, so that His sheep would not face death. Even the Old Testament saints knew that the blood of bulls and goats simply represented the ultimate sacrifice Who was coming soon.

As we thank the Lord for our daily bread and His abundant blessings, it is good to rejoice in the greatest of all blessings—we have been given eternal life through His shed blood. The cup of wine over which Christ gave *euchar* represents the *thusia* (slaughtered animal), which prompts an outpouring of thanksgiving!

Lord, help us offer up thanks for the fact that You were slaughtered in our place. And, Father, may we learn to give thanks for the sacrificial places to which You sometimes call us as believers.

The Wardrobe of Heaven

*On His robe and thigh was written
this title: King of Kings and Lord of Lords.*
—Revelation 19:16

The Scripture focuses often on garments. For example, when the King of Kings entered the world the first time, He was "wrapped in swaddling clothes, lying in a manger." He came as a dependent baby, in the dark of night, dressed in torn rags, "strips of cloth."

Again, when the King of Kings was crucified on the cross, rejected, scorned, and humiliated, the soldiers stripped Him naked and "cast lots" for His garments.

Yet another defining moment in world history is due to unfold at any moment. Christ has promised to return, visibly, as the conquering King. The apostle John was given a clear vision of the precise details of this scene.

When the Lord returns He will be mounted on a white horse, not astride a humble donkey. His eyes will be as flames of fire. On His head will be many crowns. Out of His mouth will be seen a sharp, glistening sword, a symbol of the Word of God with which He will deliver the wrath of God on all unbelievers. His robe will be blood-stained, a reminder of Who He is: the Lamb of God, slain for the sins of all who believe. Written on this blood-stained robe and engraved on His thigh will be His name: King of Kings and Lord of Lords (Read Revelation 19:11-16).

This is the manner in which Christ will return, no longer to bring salvation, but rather to bring judgment upon all the kings of the earth and all who have refused to call Him Lord in this life.

Interestingly, "the armies of heaven" will come with Christ, also upon white horses. They will be "clothed in fine linen, white and clean" (Revelation 19:14). It is clear that those who are a part of this King's army must also have special clothing. These white robes symbolize the sinlessness of those who are followers of the King of Kings. The King Himself has provided their clothing: "I will greatly rejoice in the Lord...for He has clothed me with the garments of salvation. He has covered me with the robe of righteousness" (Isaiah 61:10).

As we await the arrival of the King, it is good to examine the "clothing" we are wearing. The prophet Isaiah tells us that "all our righteousnesses are as filthy rags" (Isaiah 64:6). In other words, all our human efforts and good works will not get us ready to greet the One coming to judge the world. Rather, He must provide us with the "garment" of salvation, the cleansing of His blood shed for our sins.

Very few were prepared for the first arrival of the King wrapped in rags. Most rejected Him and were part of a crucifying crowd. He is about to appear again, unexpectedly, "like a thief in the night" to those who do not know Him. His name will be in clear view on His garments, King of Kings and Lord of Lords.

"Even so, come Lord Jesus" (Revelation 22:20).

The Prince of Peace

His Name shall be called Wonderful,
Counselor, The Mighty God,
The Everlasting Father, The Prince of Peace.
—Isaiah 9:6b

This is a startling Scripture if we actually read it and believe it. The first half of the verse is so familiar to us that we often don't hear or believe the last half. "For unto us a Child is born, a Son is given...and His name shall be called...." The name of Jesus Christ, this Child, born of the virgin, is "the mighty God." Christ's name is God. And Christ's name is "the everlasting Father."

The Lord Himself confirmed this again and again as He walked on earth. "If you have seen me, you have seen the Father" (John 14:9). "The Father and I are One" (John 10:30). "Before Abraham was born I existed" (John 8:58). Christ is the visible reality of the Lord God of Israel, Creator of heaven and earth (John 1:18).

Practically speaking, what do these names of Jesus Christ mean to us? Certainly we can rejoice every single hour if we understand Christ is indeed God. This light alone is a miraculous gift that will keep us grateful day after day.

Yet there is much more. His name is also Prince of Peace. The Hebrew word for peace is *shalom*. It means safe, well, happy, friendly, prospering, and healthy.

The Greek word for peace is *eirene*, which implies rest, quietness, prosperity, well-being. In today's world most people are longing for a sense of well-being. "I just want to be happy." "I'd just like some peace, some security." "I'd like to get some rest." Maybe we are looking for peace in all the wrong places.

The Hebrew word for prince is *sar*. (In Russian, it is czar!) It means the captain, the ruler, the commander, the one who reigns over and is in charge of a realm. Christ is the One in charge of peace! He reigns over the realm called Peace. If you or I want to live in that realm, we have to go to the *sar* and ask to walk in His realm, under His dominion, living within the truths of the kingdom of peace!

The apostle Paul tells us that Christ is our peace (Ephesians 2:14). In Christ all of our concerns are lifted; all of our needs are met. Because He is King over the realm of peace, He knows how to solve all problems; He is never faced with the "unexpected;" He has a perfect plan for every citizen in His realm. And this plan is designed for our highest good. He has written our days in a book (Psalm 139). Our steps are ordained (Proverbs 16:9). He loves us completely, in spite of our failures, inadequacies, bad habits, and lack of trust.

Because Paul understood these realities, he could confidently write, "Don't worry about anything; instead, pray about everything.... If you do this, you will experience God's peace, which is far more wonderful than the human mind can understand" (Philippians 4:6-7 NLT).

Are we living in the realm of the Prince of Peace because we are alive in Christ? If so, are we experiencing the peace that is supernatural, the peace that defies the circumstances we might be facing? It is this kind of peace the Prince provides. The key is to believe the *sar* has everything in perfect order and will faithfully work out the details of our lives.

Lord, please deliver the experience of Your peace to our hearts by Your Spirit.

God's Sovereignty in the Details

*And in the sixth month the angel Gabriel was sent from
God unto a city of Galilee,
named Nazareth, to a virgin,
and the virgin's name was Mary.*
—Luke 1:26-27

It is fascinating to discover the tiny details that hide behind the surface of biblical truth. Here we have a familiar quote from Luke chapter one. Let's ask ourselves this question: In the sixth month of what? If we return to Luke chapter one, we discover that it is the sixth month of Elizabeth's pregnancy.

Who is Elizabeth? Elizabeth is the wife of a Jewish priest named Zacharias. Elizabeth, who had been barren for some time, has been blessed with becoming pregnant after Zacharias' fervent prayer. And the coming birth of this child is announced by an angel (Luke 1:11-13) and the angel's name is Gabriel (Luke 1:19).

What was so special about this baby that an angelic announcement was given? The angel himself tells us the answer.

This child's name will be John and he will be filled with the Holy Spirit before he is even born (Luke 1:13-15).

Why was John going to be so important? Because he was going to be the one to go throughout all of Israel and trumpet the news that the Messiah had been born; he would "make ready a people prepared for the Lord." His name, of course, is John the Baptist (Luke 1:15-17).

Interesting, isn't it, that it was this same angel, Gabriel, who brought the news of pregnancy to Mary (Luke 1:26). When Mary discovered she was pregnant (and not married), she "went into the hill country" to visit her cousin Elizabeth. The angel Gabriel had told Mary that her cousin Elizabeth, who was very old, was also pregnant. In fact, she was six months' pregnant (Luke 1:35-40).

Isn't the Lord's timing amazing? He made sure Elizabeth remained barren so that when she did become pregnant she would clearly see the hand of God at work. And the Lord planned the timing so that Jesus' second cousin, John the Baptist, would be just six months older than He, so John could announce the arrival of the Lamb of God (John 1:29).

What a special gift the Lord gave these two women. He ordained the timing of their miraculous pregnancies; He gave them angelic visitations; He knit their destinies together; He made certain they were born within the same family tree so they would be cousins. God is sovereign and gracious. These two women must have shared so much and been so grateful for each other's company and the confirmation of the Lord's hand in their lives.

Finally, isn't it interesting that Elizabeth was a descendant of Aaron, the high priest who served with Moses? She was named after Aaron's wife whose name, in Greek, was Elizabeth. Mary was named after Aaron's sister Miriam, whose name in Greek is Mary. The Lord sends us signals in the Word that He is the God of all the details, even the details of our daily lives.

Oh, sovereign God, give us eyes to see Your hand in every detail of our days and nights, in every season of our lives. Glorify Your name in us.

Spotless!

There is no spot in thee....
—Song of Solomon 4:7

There exists the mythical idea that because God is loving He will be generous when judging sin. It is believed by most that God basically grades on a curve. There are some really bad people in the world so, if hell exists, those people will go there. But others of us are not really that awful, so, if heaven exists, we will qualify. Especially because we believe in God, sometimes pray, and mostly try to do the right thing.

Sound familiar? Seems logical, doesn't it? Yet that entire philosophy or outlook is totally based on human reasoning. It is completely unbiblical and has its source in the enemy of God, the great deceiver, who twists the Word of God.

In the Old Testament sacrificial system, the lamb or heifer that was chosen as the sacrifice had to be "without blemish," "without spot." "Bring thee a red heifer, without spot" (Numbers 19:2). Jesus Christ was announced as the sacrificial Lamb of God by John the Baptist. Christ's death on the cross was the blood sacrifice. "He offered Himself without spot to God" (Hebrews 9:14).

Again, in the Old Testament, leprosy is described as "a freckled spot that groweth" (Leviticus 13:39). A leper was considered unclean and sent "outside the camp." Leprosy became a symbol, biblically, of sin. Whether a leper had just a spot or was completely ravaged by the disease, he or she was counted as unclean. When Jesus healed lepers in His ministry, they were described as being "cleansed" (Mark 8:3).

How does this relate to us? The Word of God says every person who expects to be received of God must be "without spot, unrebukable" (1 Timothy 6:14). Those presented to Jesus Christ in heaven are described as "not having spot, or wrinkle… but must be holy and without blemish" (Ephesians 5:27).

It is clear from the Scripture that God does not grade on a curve. Not even a blemish, not one spot of sin will enter heaven. And this is why the gospel is, in Greek, the *euaggellion*, the declaration of good news.

Evangelism is simply the declaration of the greatest good news on the face of the earth or in the heavenly spheres. Christ, the spotless One, has paid the price for our spots, our sin. And He rose from the grave to prove His victory over sin and death. "This is life eternal that they might know Thee, the only True God, and Jesus Christ, whom Thou has sent" (John 17:3).

When the Spirit of God opens our eyes to this incredible truth—that only through faith in Christ are we counted worthy of heaven—we begin to grasp the monumental significance of being a believer.

It is to those of us who are in Christ, born again by His Spirit (John 3:7-8), that the Lord Himself speaks these amazing words: "There is no spot in thee" (Song of Solomon 4:7).

In the poetic symbolism of the Song of Solomon love story, Christ is the Bridegroom speaking to His bride, the church, the body of true believers. He says, "You are so beautiful, my beloved, so perfect in every part.... How sweet is your love, my treasure, my bride..." (Song of Solomon 4:7, 10 NLT).

The apostle Paul used this same imagery to describe the believer's relationship with the Lord. In speaking of Christ's love for the church, depicted as His bride, the apostle wrote, "He gave up his life for her to make her holy and clean.... He did this to present her to himself...without a spot or wrinkle or any other blemish" (Ephesians 5:25-27 NLT).

Lord, we fall before Your throne in gratefulness, knowing that You deem us as spotless because You, the Lamb without blemish, have made it to be so. Hallelujah!

Heaven

Behold, the heaven and the heaven of heavens
belong to the Lord thy God....
—Deuteronomy 10:14a

What Do We Know about Heaven?

In the beginning God created the heaven and the earth.
—*Genesis 1:1*

It is amazing to me to realize that heaven is a created place, separate from the Creator. God Himself is so majestic, so infinite, so incomprehensible that He is not limited to a place called heaven, though we know the Scripture says He is indeed in heaven (and beyond heaven) and on earth residing in the believer! Theologians, of course, call that God's omnipresence. "Behold, the heaven and heaven of heavens cannot contain Thee" (1 Kings 8:27).

Sometimes it seems refreshing to ponder anew some biblical passages and enhance our sense of awe about all that we do not know or really comprehend regarding the majesty of the Lord and the mysteries in His Word.

For example, another shocking biblical proclamation is that heaven has an ending. Heaven has a beginning, and heaven will come to an end. Jesus described His coming to earth again and said that at that time, "Heaven and earth shall pass away..." (Matthew 24:35).

The apostle Peter gave us a few more details. "Looking for and hasting unto the coming of the day of God, wherein the heavens being on fire shall be dissolved and the elements shall melt with fervent heat" (2 Peter 3:12).

The Hebrew word for heaven is *shamayim* and is a plural word, heavens. There are at least three heavens. They include the open expanse above the earth (the firmament), the realm of the celestial bodies (the sun, moon, stars, planets) and then the place where God is revealed (but not contained) in His glory. The apostle Paul described being "caught up to the third heaven" and seeing the glories of God (2 Corinthians 12:2).

Paul also told us that Christ "ascended up far above all heavens that He might fill all things" (Ephesians 4:10). Can our minds even imagine somewhere beyond heaven? In Hebrews we read that Christ is our High Priest and has been made "higher than the heavens" (Hebrews 7:26).

Oh, the magnitude of the One we worship. "Eye has not seen nor ear heard...the things God has prepared" for those of us who love Him (1 Corinthians 2:9). And to stretch us even further, our Creator has promised to create a new heaven and a new earth after the first heaven and the first earth are gone (Revelation 21:1).

Help us, oh, Lord, to grasp how incomprehensible You are. May our awe be enlarged. And may we rejoice to think You have ordained us as believers to share in Your glory, which extends beyond heaven!

The Heavenly Roll Call

These names all come from ancient records.
—1 Chronicles 4:22 NLT

Isn't it amazing to see how the Word of God scrupulously records the names of people? There are long lists of people and families, especially in the Old Testament. As we read these, they can often seem boring and somewhat useless.

But I believe the Lord is sending us a very important love message through these "ancient records." An "ancient record" of names determines our eternal destiny. Christ told the disciples that the single most important joy-producing fact of their entire existence was to know that their names were written in heaven (Luke 10:20).

The Lamb's Book of Life records the names of all those for whom Christ died. Paul described his coworkers in the gospel as those "whose names are in the book of life" (Philippians 4:3).

This eternal life is the inheritance of the saints, those who have discovered Jesus Christ to be God in the flesh. Peter described this inheritance as "reserved in heaven for you" (1 Peter 1:4).

This Book of Life, the ancient record of the names of those who will live in heaven forever, was written "from the foundation of the world" (Revelation 13:8). This list of names is the most critical, incredible, important roll call in the universe!

The names of all the lost sheep whom the Shepherd has promised to find are on this list. Jesus tells us in John 10:3 that the Shepherd "calleth his own sheep by name." The sheep know His voice. The Shepherd gives His life for His sheep (John 10:12, 15). He knows His sheep. He is not willing that one of His sheep should perish (Matthew 18:14). Christ explains that He has come for the express purpose of saving these lost sheep whose names are in the record book (Matthew 18:11). He has promised to find each and every one. Not one whose name is in the book will be lost. He taught that clearly in the parable of the ninety-nine sheep as the shepherd sought the last sheep, number one hundred. The entire flock was shown to be saved and protected.

As Peter wrote, we are being "returned unto the Shepherd and Bishop" of our souls (1 Peter 2:25). This is, of course, the Lord Himself, the very Shepherd who chose us "before the foundation of the world" (Ephesians 1:4).

Oh Lord, let us treasure this "ancient record." We fall down at Your feet in utter gratefulness as we discover You as Lord of all, and the One Who has found us and known us before the world began and placed us in Your ancient record.

He Looked for a City

He looked for a city which has foundations,
whose builder and maker is God.
—Hebrews 11:10

Abraham, the patriarch, is the epitome of what it means to live by faith. Abraham simply believed the Word of God and left his home and country to follow the Lord. "He went without knowing where he was going" (Hebrews 11:8 NLT).

But we discover that Abraham had a destination; he had a vision of what his destination would look like. That vision sustained him during the years his faith was being tested. He knew he was on a journey to a city built by God Himself.

In the passage from Hebrews 11:10, the original Greek says "He looked for the city..." not just a city. The city is the capital of a country. Those who live by faith are said to be seeking a country as well as a city. The saints of old "confessed that they were strangers and pilgrims on the earth...they desire a better country, that is a heavenly one…and God has prepared for them a city" (Hebrews 11:13, 16).

Faith is about believing in what we cannot see physically, but what we know to be true in the invisible realm. In fact, because we are living in a realm over which Satan currently reigns (2 Corinthians 4:4), much of what appears to be real is pure deception.

If we know Christ, then we, too, are to be looking for the city. The city is the city of God, Jerusalem, the city of Zion. This city exists right now, at this very moment. No wonder Abraham looked for the city "which hath foundations." He must have seen the city. "And I saw the holy city, the new Jerusalem coming down from God out of heaven…. It sparkled like a precious gem…. The wall of the city was built on foundation stones inlaid with twelve gems" (Revelation 21:2, 11, 19 NLT).

The psalmist experienced pure joy when he thought about his destination. "On the holy mountain stands the city of Jerusalem…. O city of God, what glorious things are said of you!" (Psalm 87:1-3 NLT).

The prophet Ezekiel, while in exile, saw the city of God. "The heavens were opened to me, and I saw visions of God… and I felt the hand of the Lord take a hold of me" (Ezekiel 1:1, 3 NLT). He went on to say, "The Lord took a hold of me…he took me to the land of Israel and set me down on a very high mountain. From there I could see what appeared to be a city…" (Ezekiel 40:1-2 NLT). Ezekiel then described the city in detail over the next eight chapters of his book. At one point he wrote, "And the Lord said to me, 'Son of man, this is the place of my throne and the place where I will rest my feet. I will remain here forever…'" (Ezekiel 43:7 NLT).

The Lord Himself spoke of this place to the disciples, "Let not your heart be troubled.... In My Father's house are many mansions [abiding places in Greek].... I go to prepare a place for you. I will come again, and receive you unto myself, that where I am, there you may be also" (John 14:1-3).

Isn't it interesting that the Lord suggests that one of the significant elements in not having a "troubled heart" is to focus on the place to which we are going? Paul knew this to be true. "If you then be risen with Christ, seek those things which are above, where Christ sits on the right hand of God. Set your affection on things above, not on things on this earth...when Christ, who is our life, shall appear, then you also shall appear with Him in glory" (Colossians 3:1-2, 4).

How much time each day do we spend thinking about the incredible joy ahead of us? Do we really believe the city exists, complete with diamond-studded walls and gates of solid pearl? Do we picture the future that is ours, living in that awareness, hour by hour and day by day? Our joy level is in direct proportion to our continual awareness of our true home, the country of heaven.

The Scripture says we have been born "from above," we are citizens of heaven. "And of Zion it shall be said, 'This and that man was born in her' [Jerusalem, the city of Zion]... the Lord shall count, when He writes up the people, 'This man was born there'" (Psalm 87:5-6).

The apostle Paul said that the heavenly city, Jerusalem, is the "mother" of all believers (Galatians 4:26). This is our true home. Our inheritance is stored in the city. We have been born into an inheritance that is "incorruptible...reserved in heaven for you...ready to be revealed in the last time" (1 Peter 1:3-5).

The author of Hebrews described the faith of Abraham and numerous saints, naming them one by one (Hebrews chapter 11), who were headed for "Mount Zion, unto the city of the living God, the heavenly Jerusalem, to an innumerable company of angels, to the general assembly and church of the firstborn which are written in heaven…and to Jesus…" (Hebrews 12:22-24).

Lord, help us live today in the vivid hope of our certain future. Help us, like Abraham, to live by faith in Your promise regarding our glorious destination.

Heavenly Beings, Not Earth Dwellers

*Having been born again, not of corruptible seed,
but of incorruptible....*
—*1 Peter 1:23*

Most of us know at least a little about our family heritage. If you have an Italian background, you may well tend to talk with your hands. If you have a little Scottish in your genes, you may be prone to pinching pennies. Our DNA heritage impacts us in the here and now.

The apostle Peter gave us the truth about our spiritual heritage in this verse, describing how we were born again. This heritage is far more significant than our flesh and blood heritage. Peter provided shocking information. He said, "You have been born of incorruptible sperm!" The Greek word for seed is *spora*, which literally means sperm. We have been "born from above;" our true Father is in heaven. We have His DNA, the divine nature infused in us by the Holy Spirit. If we are in Christ, we are no longer earthlings!

Oh, to grasp what this means to us as we live with our feet still standing on the clay of earth!

1 Peter 1:23 (NLT) says, "For you have been born again. Your new life did not come from your earthly parents because the life they gave you will end in death. But this new life will last forever because it comes from the eternal, living word of God."

The believers of the first century seemed to have had a clear grasp on their heavenly citizenship. They were focused on the "new life" they had received, which had transformed them from being mortals. They lived with a concrete awareness of being new creations, heavenly beings.

Paul, like Peter, talked about this "new life." "Since you have been raised to new life with Christ, set your sights on the realities of heaven.... Let heaven fill your thoughts. Do not think only about things down here on earth. For you died when Christ died and your real life is hidden with Christ in God" (Colossians 3:1-3 NLT).

We are urged to live with a completely different mindset than that of earth dwellers. We are heavenly beings. Our life is in heaven now. "We are seated with Him in the heavenly realms" (Ephesians 2:6 NLT).

What would we do differently if we were to live like the heavenly beings we are? Earth dwellers are preoccupied with worry. They worry about money, jobs, their future, their health, their children, etc. They experience frustration, anger, bitterness, despair, self-pity. And most of these negative elements are a result of fear of not being able to control their circumstances, unable to create a comfortable life for themselves.

In contrast, the Lord Himself explains the life experience of those who are citizens of heaven whose feet are still on earth.

In Matthew 6 He teaches us, "No one can serve two masters.... So I tell you, don't worry about everyday life.... Can all your worries add a single moment to your life?.... Why be like the pagans who are so deeply concerned about these things? Your heavenly Father already knows all your needs..." (Matthew 6:24-25, 27, 32 NLT).

Perhaps we do not really believe what the Lord says about us. He says we are born from above; we are His children. We have a mansion and an inheritance reserved for us in heaven. Heaven is our destination. We are only momentarily spending a little time walking alongside earth dwellers.

Our spiritual heritage includes wealth, purpose, and eternal reward. We have a Father Who is actively working everything in our lives together for good. Nothing can separate us from His love, mercy, care, and plan for us. Do we live each day in the peace of these realities?

The apostle Paul encouraged us to live in this peace. "Remember, the Lord is coming soon. Don't worry about anything; instead, pray about everything. Tell God what you need, and thank him for all He has done. If you do this, you will experience God's peace, which is far more wonderful than the human mind can understand" (Philippians 4:5b, 6 NLT).

Lord, please give us the grace and wisdom to live like who we are.

Do You Know the Name of God?

I will set him on high because he hath known My Name.
—Psalm 91:14

Here is the only qualification for heaven—to know the name of God. Sounds simple, doesn't it? Yet we realize that there are many who claim to know God, who call Him Lord, who do good works in His name, yet Jesus says He never knew them (Matthew 7:21-23).

The Hebrew word for knowing is *yada*, and it means to ascertain by seeing. Yet we know Jesus often chided those who had eyes to see but could "see not." In Luke 24, after His resurrection, Jesus appeared to two disciples walking on the road to Emmaus. He visited with them, "But they didn't know who he was, because God kept them from recognizing him" (Luke 24:16 NLT).

The Lord then began to teach them from the Word of God, teaching them what the Old Testament says about the Messiah, the name of God in the flesh. "Then Jesus quoted passages from the writings of Moses and all the prophets, explaining what all the Scriptures said about himself" (Luke 24:27 NLT).

Jesus went home with them to spend the night. "As they sat down to eat, he took a small loaf of bread, asked God's blessing on it, broke it, then gave it to them. Suddenly their eyes were opened, and they recognized him" (Luke 24:30-31 NLT). The King James Version reads, "their eyes were opened and they knew him." The Greek word for knew is *epiginosko,* which means to be fully acquainted with, having an intimate relationship.

It becomes clear that seeing and knowing Who God is unfolds as a result of the miracle of revelation. God uses His Word to bring this revelation. Human eyes, human wisdom, cannot know the name of the Lord. "God in his wisdom saw to it that the world would never find him through human wisdom…"(1 Corinthians 1:21 NLT).

In Christ's prayer to the Father we find the secret for knowing the name of God. Speaking of Himself, Jesus said, "For you have given him authority over everyone in all the earth. He gives eternal life to each one you have given him. And this is the way to have eternal life – to know you, the only true God, and Jesus Christ, the one you sent to earth" (John 17:2-3).

Only those whom the Father has given to the Son as love gifts know God's name. "I have manifested Thy Name unto the men which Thou gavest Me out of the world: Thine they were, and Thou gavest them Me" (John 17:6). The Lord told His disciples, "You are permitted to understand the secrets about the Kingdom of God. But I am using these stories to conceal everything about it from outsiders" (Mark 4:11).

271

The reason eternal life is such a gift is that not everyone has had the Holy Spirit open their eyes to see that Jesus Christ is God. "For there is none other name under heaven given among men, whereby we must be saved" (Acts 4:12).

We will be "set on high" to reign with Him forever because He has revealed His name to us. If we are among those who confess Jesus as Lord of heaven and earth, we can know we have received this miraculous revelation. Let us rejoice and be glad!

Oh Lord, continue to open the eyes of our hearts that we might see You more fully.

Set Your Mind on Things Above

*Since you have been raised to new life with Christ,
set your sights on the realities of heaven, where
Christ sits at God's right hand in the place of honor and power.
Let heaven fill your thoughts. Do not think only
about things down here on earth.*
—*Colossians 3:1-2 NLT*

Paul exhorts us to think about heaven. It is difficult, however, to think about things we haven't seen or experienced. Perhaps it would help if we considered the clues given by those who have been to heaven and returned to earth to tell us about it.

Paul had seen heaven firsthand. He wrote of this experience in 2 Corinthians 12:1-8. He heard the Lord speaking there. It was such a glorious place he could not find the words to describe what he saw and heard.

It is interesting that when Paul tried to describe the grandeur of heaven he quoted the prophet Isaiah who had also seen into heaven (Isaiah 6:1-13). Paul's account of heaven agreed with Isaiah's account. "No eye has seen, no ear has heard, and no mind has imagined what God has prepared for those who love him"

(1 Corinthians 2:9 NLT). Then Paul said a very strange thing, "But we know these things because God has revealed them to us by His Spirit..." (1 Corinthians 2:10 NLT). He was saying that these secret things of God come to us by revelation. In other words, we can read the Scriptural accounts of heaven, and the Holy Spirit will apply the truths of His Word so that we can get a concrete glimpse of what our heavenly future holds for us!

The apostle John was lifted up to see heaven also (Revelation chapter 4). He gave us more concrete information. "The city was pure gold, as clear as glass. The wall of the city was built on foundation stones inlaid with twelve gems...the twelve gates were made of pearls—each gate from a single pearl! And the main street was pure gold as clear as glass" (Revelation 21:19-21 NLT). John was describing the incredible capital city (the New Jerusalem) of the country of heaven. In addition, he described the multitude of angels, the sounds he heard, and the amazing creatures he saw. We begin to catch a glimpse of the beauty, the magnificence of heaven, through John.

Moses and Elijah have both been in heaven for thousands of years. And these two heavenly citizens came to earth and visited with Peter, James, and John (Matthew chapter 17). They appeared in physical flesh and bone bodies. (Jesus, of course, rose from the dead in a flesh and bone body.) Moses and Elijah carried on meaningful conversations using language the disciples apparently could understand. Their physical bodies, though flesh and bone, were not subject to gravity. They could descend and ascend freely. (Jesus ascended, free from gravity, in Acts chapter 1.)

Perhaps it was through his experience with Jesus as well as with Moses and Elijah that John could tell us, "But we know that when he [Christ] comes we will be like him, for we will see him as he really is" (1 John 3:2 NLT). John told us that our heavenly bodies and experience will be just like Christ's.

Jesus Himself came down from heaven and taught us how to "set our minds on things above." In Matthew chapter six, we read about what our mindset will be like as we focus on our eternal future. Christ summarizes these truths by saying, "So don't worry about having enough food or drink or clothing. Why be like the pagans who are so deeply concerned about these things? Your heavenly Father already knows all your needs, and he will give you all you need from day to day if you live for him and make the Kingdom of God your primary concern. So don't worry about tomorrow…" (Matthew 6:31-34 NLT).

Lord, help us focus on the heavenly realities, knowing we will dwell there forever with You.

We Shall Reign
with Him

If we suffer, we shall also reign with Him.
—2 Timothy 2:12

The Greek word translated reign in the New Testament is *basileuo*, which means "to be a king." In Revelation 11:15 we read, "The kingdoms of this world are become the kingdom of our Lord, and of His Christ; and He shall reign for ever and ever." This is a description of the Lord coming to reign as King of Kings.

In the Timothy passage above, Paul said that as believers, though we will suffer here on earth, "we shall reign with Him." The Greek word used to express this reigning is *sumbasileuo*, which means to reign together with Jesus Christ.

The apostle John saw a vision of the future as the Lord revealed the end of earth as we know it. He described the saints and said, "You have caused them to become God's kingdom and his priests and they will reign on earth" (Revelation 5:10 NLT).

How much time, in our day-to-day living, do we think about what our eternal future will be like? Sometimes it seems we get caught up in the world's focus on the here and now, desiring more material wealth or envying those who seem to have "made it to the top." This kind of focus is a joy-stealer, causing us to become greedy, jealous, or angry about what we don't have.

Sometimes it is helpful to turn our eyes upon the future that is ours. We own everything in heaven and earth, even now, because He does. All the riches of creation, all the gold, silver, and precious stones, are ours, even now. We simply do not yet have access to this abundance.

Again and again the New Testament describes the "unsearchable riches" that are ours in Christ, "the glory of His inheritance in the saints" (Ephesians 1:18, 3:8). And this inheritance is "reserved in heaven" for you (1 Peter 1:4).

Peter described another reward "reserved" for those who are deceived, "having eyes full of adultery…unstable souls; a heart exercised with covetous practices…they speak great swelling words of vanity…they allure through the lusts of the flesh" (2 Peter 2:12-18). The reward, the inheritance of earth dwellers who are outside of Christ, is the wrath of God.

Lord, help us to live each day with the awareness of who we are in You. Protect us from the alluring, beguiling world of the enemy (2 Corinthians 4:4). Cause us to see that any current suffering is nothing compared to the coming glory to which You have appointed us.

The Riches of God's Glory

*And that He might make known the riches of
His glory on the vessels of mercy,
which He had afore prepared unto glory, even us,
whom He hath called....*
—Romans 9:23-24

Can we even begin to grasp what "the riches of God's glory" would be? Paul told us that we, the called (those who have come to Christ by faith) are the ones through whom "the riches of His glory" will be displayed.

God's glory is the very essence of God. Whenever God reveals Himself, His glory is what is seen. John wrote, "Yes, dear friends, we are already God's children, and we can't even imagine what we will be like when Christ returns. But we do know that when He comes we will be like Him..." (1 John 3:2 NLT). In other words, the essence of God, the richness of His glory as expressed in Christ, will be visible in us!

Paul revealed this truth in his letter to the Ephesians. He explained that we have been resurrected with Christ to a new life, seated even now with Him in the heavenlies, so "that in the ages to come He might show the exceeding riches of His grace in His kindness toward us…" (Ephesians 2:6-7).

Again, Paul elaborated on this amazing reality in Ephesians chapter three. "I was chosen to explain to everyone this plan…. God's purpose was to show His wisdom in all its rich variety to all the rulers and authorities in the heavenly realms" (Ephesians 3:8-9 NLT).

The Lord, in His manifold wisdom, devised a plan by which He would display His character to the entire universe. He created this plan before the foundation of the world. As we read in Romans 9:23, "…which He had afore prepared unto glory…."

Central to His plan is the revelation of the richness of His grace. This will become visible when He reveals that He has chosen you and me, lumps of clay, to be vessels of His mercy. The glorious kindness and mercy of God toward us as sinners will confound the angels, the unbelievers, the demons—all the onlookers in God's entire creation—forever, in all "the ages to come."

This is our destiny, our true purpose for existing. We are alive in Christ for the ultimate purpose of being eternal trophies or testimonies of His goodness toward us as sinners.

Some days we get this backwards. We believe it is our goodness He is interested in having displayed. No. It is "the riches of His glory," His grace, His mercy, His kindness, His goodness that will be on display. He is creating His life in us through the sanctifying work of His Spirit.

Our practical daily response is to join the apostle Paul who wrote, "That He would grant you, according to the riches of

His glory, to be strengthened with might by His Spirit..." (Ephesians 3:16).

Father, grant us the ability to see that You alone will be glorified in the ages to come; help us see that all that is unfolding in our lives is for Your glory.

This World and that World

And Jesus answering said unto them, "The children of this world marry, and are given in marriage: But they which shall be accounted worthy to obtain that world, and the resurrection from the dead, neither marry, nor are given in marriage. Neither can they die any more: for they are equal unto the angels; and are the children of God, being the children of the resurrection.
—Luke 20:34-36

The Lord has revealed some amazing truths to us in this simple teaching. He refers to "this world" and then to "that world." He makes it clear that these two "worlds" are quite different. Those who are worthy to obtain "that world" will be like the angels in the sense that they will live forever and earthly institutions like marriage will not exist. (As an aside, remember that the purpose of marriage is procreation according to Genesis 1:27-28. The Lord is not suggesting that in "that world" we won't have very special relationships of love with those we have known here on earth.)

What is the Lord telling us in this Luke passage? The Greek word for world is *aion*, which means age or a duration of time. There are many different periods of time, or ages, which the

Lord has prepared and arranged in His eternal plan. Each age is unique and defined by His decree.

In Matthew 12:32 the Lord says there is no forgiveness in this world (*aion*, age) or in the world (*aion*, age) to come for those who resist the Holy Spirit. In Hebrews 11:3 we learn that the worlds (*aions*, ages) were framed (prepared) by the Word of God. Thus, we are currently living in a God-ordained age unlike the age to come.

Paul told us in Ephesians 1:21 that Christ reigns over all things "not only in this world (*aion*, age) but also in that which is to come."

In Matthew 13:49 Jesus describes what it will be like at the "end of this world." He has given us signs of His return and "of the end of the world" (Matthew 24:3.). The Lord clearly teaches that one of the aspects of the world to come is that those who enter that age will have eternal life (Mark 10:30). Interestingly, the Greek word for eternal is *aionian*. In this next age (*aion*), those who enter will be eternal (*aionian*) beings!

Satan is the "god of this world" (2 Corinthians 4:4). "This world" is filled with "cares" and "deceitfulness." Paul said that Christ gave Himself for our sins that He might deliver us from this present evil world.

Obviously "this world" is not our home if we are "children of the resurrection." We are those who are "accounted worthy" to reign with the Lord in the coming age. We are "worthy" because, through the gift of faith, we are hidden "in Christ in God" (Colossians 3:3). Because of His worthiness, we are counted worthy of eternal (*aionian*) life. "Worthy is the Lamb that was slain" (Revelation 5:12).

Because we will reign in the age to come, we are to be "look-ing for that blessed [happy] hope, and the glorious appearing of the great God and our Savior Jesus Christ" (Titus 2:13).

Lord, lift up our eyes by Your grace. May we see You. Free us from focusing on the things of this world.

The End of the Age

But now once in the end of the world hath He appeared
to put away sin by the sacrifice of Himself.
—Hebrews 9:26

The Scripture says Christ appeared now and now is described as "the end of the world" in the King James Version. Yet two thousand years have passed and "the end of the world" seems not to have come.

It helps to know that the Greek version actually reads "in the end of the ages." In other words, we are in the end of a series of ages or *aions* in which God has been revealing Himself. We live in the end of the ages that shared some things in common. For example, all humans throughout all the ages since man was created have been mortals. They have the sin nature, and the wages of sin is death.

Yet in the coming age, believers will have immortal bodies. We will never die. Rather, we will be reigning with Christ over a new and unique dispensation or age. We will have purpose, specific assignments. We will function as priests with access to the very throne of God (Revelation 1:6). The cares of this world will no longer exist for us (Matthew 13:22).

The Scripture even describes our physical appearance in the coming age. We will shine like the sun (Matthew 13:43). We will appear to be "arrayed in fine linen, clean and white." Christ's righteousness will shine through us and our appearance will be like white light. And the Lord's name will be written on our foreheads (Revelation 22:4).

We tend to say, "I think all of that is just symbolism, and it doesn't have any practical value for me in the here and now." Yet the New Testament writers found these realities to be the very essence of their daily joy and strength. They had their minds set on the kingdom to come.

The disciples were eager to know when the end of this age would come. Jesus went into great detail so they would look for the coming kingdom (Matthew 24). He encouraged them to "watch" for this coming kingdom (Matthew 24:42). He taught parables of warning about those who were not focused on and prepared for this coming kingdom. (Five of the ten virgins were not prepared in Matthew 25.)

The apostle Paul continually urged the saints to set their minds on things above. He wrote, "Let us watch and be sober" (1 Thessalonians 5:6). Again he asked, "For what is our hope, or joy, or crown of rejoicing?" He answered that the hope and joy of his life is seeing the saints gathered at the Lord's coming. Paul's daily joy was in gathering people into the coming kingdom (1 Thessalonians 2:19-20).

The Lord's brother, Jude, instructed the saints on how to live their daily lives. He wrote, "Build yourselves up in your faith…keep looking for this eternal life that is coming to you" (Jude 20, 21).

Peter told the saints to rejoice even in their troubles because "when His glory shall be revealed" you will have exceeding joy (1 Peter 4:13). Peter knew that the practical way to get through our challenges is to stay focused on the coming kingdom when Christ will be revealed and the saints will be glorified.

Peter went on to urge the saints to be "looking for" the coming of the day of the Lord. We are to "look for" the new heavens and the new earth. "Wherefore, beloved, seeing that ye look for such things, be diligent…" (2 Peter 3:12-14).

Oh Lord, You have told us that we are not of this world, even though we are in it. Renew our hunger for the world to come so that we might live each day with greater joy and expectation in You.

Christ's Return

When He cometh in the glory of
His Father with the holy angels.
—*Mark 8:38*

When the Son of God came into the world more than two thousand years ago, He came with His earthly father present, without any visible fanfare or glory. Rather, He slept in an animal feedbox with only Mary, Joseph, and lowly shepherds in attendance, hidden from the eyes of the world. On His second visit, the Lord is going to come with worldwide fanfare and in the blinding glory of His heavenly Father.

On His first visit, the Lord came clothed in the humility of an earthly body. When He comes again He will be clothed in His shining heavenly garments, wrapped in a golden sash, His feet like fine brass, accompanied by "ten thousands times ten thousand, and thousands and thousands" angels (Revelation 1:13, 15; 5:11).

On His first visit, one angel came to a few shepherds in a field at night and announced the birth of the Savior "which is Christ the Lord" (Luke 2:8-11). His next visit will be in blazing glory on the Day of the Lord, seen by every eye around the world.

While He was still a toddler (no more than two years old), the Son of Man was visited by "wise men" from the east who came "to worship Him." These men understood this Child to be a King, King of the Jews. They brought Him gifts and fell down at His feet in adoration, "in the house" where He was with Mary, His mother (Matthew 2:1-11).

When the Lord returns as King of Kings, revealed to the entire world, all the kings and rulers on the earth will bow before Him. This will be a terrifying event for all who are alive who do not know Him. "And out of His mouth goeth a sharp sword, that with it He should smite the nations: and He shall rule them with a rod of iron. And He treadeth the winepress of the fierceness and wrath of Almighty God. And He hath on His vesture and on His thigh a name written KING OF KINGS AND LORD OF LORDS" (Revelation 19:15-16).

As we look back and consider the Lord's birth in Bethlehem, we are grateful and amazed. For those of us alive in the twenty-first century, it is perhaps even more thrilling to look forward to His next appearance. He arrived in Bethlehem in the still of a dark night; He will return again with the sound of trumpets in the blazing light of day. Are we, like the wise men of old, looking up with high expectations of seeing Him?

May we be among those who are "children of the light, and the children of the day." To those who are children of darkness, children of the night, Christ will come as a thief in the night, unexpected and unwelcomed (1 Thessalonians 5:4-5).

Father, remind us often, by Your Spirit, to look up expectantly. We welcome Your arrival.

The Heavenly City

And he showed me that great city, the holy Jerusalem...
having the glory of God, sparkling like a precious gem,
crystal clear like jasper.
—Revelation 21:10

Several references in the Scripture describe the dwelling place of the Lord. We know He is in heaven, and the capital city of heaven is the New Jerusalem. This city is in existence now. It is solid, constructed on a bejeweled foundation, "inlaid with twelve gems...jasper, sapphire, agate, emerald, onyx, carnelian, chrysolite, beryl, topaz, chrysoprase, jacinth, and amethyst" (Revelation 21:19 NLT). The city itself is "pure gold, as clear as glass" (Revelation 21:18 NLT).

All the saints through the ages have known of the existence of this city, and God Himself built it. Abraham "was confidently looking forward to a city with eternal foundations, a city designed and built by God" (Hebrews 11:10 NLT).

Imagine! The Lord Jesus Christ left that glorious city to enter this world, to be "laid in a manger," the home of animals. And as an adult, Christ had no home at all. "Foxes have dens to live in, and birds have nests, but I, the Son of Man, have no home of my own, not even a place to lay my head" (Matthew 8:20 NLT).

The saints of ancient times in the Old Testament were, in many cases, very wealthy. They had thriving businesses and large families and they occupied places of power and prestige in their communities. Noah, for example, had lived comfortably for six hundred years in a sophisticated society that had musical instruments, metal works of bronze and iron, large cities, etc. (Read Genesis 4:17-5:32.) Yet the Lord called Noah to leave all of that behind and go live in a wooden boat!

Abraham lived in the wealthy city of Ur of the Chaldees. Excavations of this city show it to have been located on the west bank of the Euphrates with fourteen- to fifteen-room homes containing elaborate furnishings. The time period was about 1900 BC. The Lord called him to leave all that behind. "So Abraham departed as the Lord had instructed him.... He took his wife, Sarai, his nephew Lot, and all his wealth…" (Genesis 12:4-5 NLT). Eventually Abraham spent his life traveling and living in tents, focused on the "heavenly city" to which he was called.

The Lord Himself taught clearly that our lives here on earth are temporal. Nothing here compares with the glory that is to be ours in the heavenly city. "Lay not up for yourselves treasures on earth, where moth and rust destroy and where thieves break in and steal" (Matthew 6:19). Instead He pointed us to "the treasures in heaven" that are not corruptible and cannot be stolen. "In My Father's house are many mansions.... I go to prepare a place for you..." (John 14:2). A Christ-built mansion awaits every believer!

Paul was caught up to heaven and actually saw the heavenly city and returned to describe it. Using the words of Isaiah, Paul wrote, "No eye has seen, no ear has heard, and no mind has imagined what God has prepared for those who love him" (1 Corinthians 2:9 NLT). The Savior left the heavenly city to be housed in a stable in order for us to be housed in heaven.

Lord, help us set our mind on things above, our true home.

To order additional copies of this book,
please visit www.redemption-press.com
Also available on Amazon.com and BarnesandNoble.com
Or by calling toll free 1-(844) 273-3336

CPSIA information can be obtained
at www.ICGtesting.com
Printed in the USA
FSHW02n2207130918
52086FS

9 781632 320780